Sports Psychology for Runners
By
Gary Barber

Note for Librarians: A cataloguing record for this book is available from Library and Archives
Canada at www.collectionscanada.ca/amicus/index-e.html
ISBN 1-4120-6556-9

Printed in Victoria, BC, Canada. Printed on paper with minimum 30% recycled fibre.
Trafford's print shop runs on "green energy" from solar, wind and other environmentally-friendly power sources.

TRAFFORD
PUBLISHING™

Offices in Canada, USA, Ireland and UK
This book was published *on-demand* in cooperation with Trafford Publishing. On-demand
publishing is a unique process and service of making a book available for retail sale to the
public taking advantage of on-demand manufacturing and Internet marketing. On-demand
publishing includes promotions, retail sales, manufacturing, order fulfilment, accounting and
collecting royalties on behalf of the author.

Book sales for North America and international:
Trafford Publishing, 6E–2333 Government St.,
Victoria, BC v8t 4p4 CANADA
phone 250 383 6864 (toll-free 1 888 232 4444)
fax 250 383 6804; email to orders@trafford.com
Book sales in Europe:
Trafford Publishing (uk) Limited, 9 Park End Street, 2nd Floor
Oxford, UK ox1 1hh UNITED KINGDOM
phone 44 (0)1865 722 113 (local rate 0845 230 9601)
facsimile 44 (0)1865 722 868; info.uk@trafford.com
Order online at:
trafford.com/05-1467

10 9 8 7 6 5 4 3

Sports Psychology for Runners

Athletes of today are increasingly recognising the power and impact of their thinking on athletic performance. They understand that there is a fine line between personal excellence and disappointment and often, it is the frame of mind that tilts a performance in a particular direction. Here is a collection of sports psychology essays that will help you to incorporate mental techniques into your training. They are presented in a non-sequential manner; i.e. you can read them in any order.

You will also find a series of stories describing the athletic achievements of some of the greatest runners in the world. These are athletes who put a human face on the sports psychology jargon, they are people who have felt sore from their training, have been anxious on the start-line, and have been confident racing to success.

Welcome to **"Sports Psychology for Runners"**! May it inspire you and bring you all the success that your hard training deserves.

Contents

Is it the thought that counts?

I've never been a great fan of that most beloved of sports clichés: "*It's all in the mind*!" or its obnoxious twin "*it's 100% mental*!" If these statements were true, I wouldn't bother running 80 miles a week and spending hours ploughing through the worst that the weather can hurl at us. Living the ultimate dream of the armchair athlete, I could just stay at home and think about it all that hard training. I could sit on my couch, massage the remote control, and maybe watch a video of the London marathon. I could keep hydrated with a six-pack of beer and think really hard about winning. And if somehow, I don't manage to win, it's only because the other athletes "*wanted it more.*"

Almost all serious athletes will, however, acknowledge that mental skill training does play at least some role in the overall preparation and delivery of a great performance. Exactly how much of an influence is hotly debated by exercise scientists, sports philosophers, and armchair experts. Let's review some of the evidence and you decide whether there is anything to this "mental stuff."

An intriguing study with direct implications for athletes was conducted by exercise scientist Bill Morgan. Morgan hypnotised cyclists before they started to cycle on a bicycle ergometer. The cyclists were asked to pedal for 15 minutes at a constant speed against a constant resistance. For the first five minutes they were told that they were cycling on a flat road. As would be expected, their heart and breathing rates increased and then plateaued. They were then told that for the next five minutes they would be cycling up a very steep hill. When this happened their heart and breathing rates dramatically increased. In the final five minute segment of the test, the cyclists were told that they were cycling on the flat road again. Their breathing and heart rates fell back down to "pre-hill" levels. Physically the task had not increased in difficulty at any time throughout the test, it was just that the cyclists believed that things were going to be harder and their bodies responded accordingly.

You have to remember that a mental skill—just like physical training—is not mastered just by doing it once. Imagine practising for a race once or twice and then saying "*the training didn't work for me, I've got to try something different.*" No serious athlete would do that with their physical training and yet, too often, mental skills are abandoned if they don't bring immediate results. The athletes who are interested in creating a mental training programme may want to consider including the following principles of training: *Frequency*—Practise on a regular basis. Just like physical training, you will need to practise regularly if you wish to see results. As you would lose fitness with extended inactivity, so you will lose the benefits of mental training without regular practise. *Duration*—Practise for a significant period (20—30 minutes per session). *Intensity*—Bring an emotional content to your practises so that you replicate (in your imagination) the race conditions. *Specificity*—Develop a range of skills that can be applied to the everchanging challenges of a running race e.g. relaxation for pre-race conditions, self control for the early stages of a race, discipline and perseverance when the race becomes physically draining. *Progression*—Improve the quality of your practises week after week.

Does mental training work?

Certainly you have to sift through the anecdotal and scientific evidence before arriving at your conclusion. Bill Rodgers—the great American marathon runner—stated that he used his mental skill training to visualize an enormous hand pushing him up the infamous HeartBreak Hill in the Boston Marathon. Was it then coincidence that Rodgers pulled away from his rivals at that critical point in his race? Then there are verified reports of deep sea divers who—using yoga techniques—have learned how slow both their heart rate (to barely a few beats per minute) and oxygen consumption rate so that they can stay under water for several minutes with only a single breath. Imagine the benefits of that kind of mental discipline in a running race: using your mind to relax a specific muscle that is repeatedly cramping toward the end of a marathon.

Further evidence of how we think and how are body responds to that thought can be found in the science of Psychoneuroimmunology. Studies have shown that white blood cells—which fight infections—function significantly better when people where given relaxation training. Also, these blood cells were found to be four times more aggressive in fighting colds when a person had positive thoughts rather than negative thoughts about the illness. Research by Richard Achterberg discovered that negative thoughts and emotions significantly increase muscular tension. As tense muscles do not work as efficiently as relaxed muscles, it is apparent how negative thinking could be to the detriment of a running performance.

Not to be outdone by the other experts, sports writers have long mined the riches of ancient philosophy looking for evidence to show that there is a connection between our thoughts, behaviour, and running performance. Aristotle believed that it was our experiences that shaped our lives: "*We are what we repeatedly do. Excellence, then is not an act but a habit.*" If Aristotle had been able to trade his toga for some lycra and entered the local 10km, he would have relied on his physical training to give him the confidence (a mental skill) needed for a great performance. Descartes would have taken a different approach. He viewed our thoughts as the main influence in our existence: "*Cogito ergo sum—I think, therefor I am!*" For him, the confidence comes first and the athlete's successful performance will then follow.

So is it the thought that counts? To help settle this debate even Shakespeare offered some advice. If you are a confident athlete bursting with energy or a nervous bag of bones remember: "*Nothing is good or bad but thinking makes it so.*"

An action packed running career

Just for a moment, I want you to imagine that a film crew has decided to make a documentary of your running career. They are with you at your first race. They record your greatest triumphs and they are with you through the setbacks. At the end of your career they take you into a cinema and roll the film. Ask yourself this question: What kind of film would you like to see? Do you believe that you are the scriptwriter of your own film? Are there planned highlights in your film, or did the best performances just occur by chance?

Setting goals is an integral part of our sport. They motivate us to practise in foul weather. They allow us to dream of the athlete we might be (a legend in our own mind?). Our sporting goals drive us to reach deeper into ourselves and ask: Can I become a better athlete? What are the limits of my abilities? If we can push ourselves hard enough can we become like pioneers charting unknown territories in search of fabulous rewards?

Just like any explorer, a runner seeking to achieve a goal, must be courageous. There may be setbacks on their journey. Adversity can come in many forms: an injury, a defeat, uncooperative weather, the list could be endless. Dealing with that adversity requires faith and confidence, an inner belief that no matter what, the goal can still be achieved; if not today, then perhaps tomorrow.

The film crew has gathered and are now preparing to film your documentary. The Director (your coach) tells you that there must be lots of action. "Action and goals you reply!"

Ready with the lights!
Roll the cameras!
A.C.T.I.O.N.!

Are your running goals measurable? Sports Psychology theory suggests that it is better to state that your goal is to run a race in a certain time rather than stating that "I just want to have a good race."

Compatible with your mission? Is your racing plan compatible with the goals that you have set for yourself for the season? Too often we can lapse into the habit of racing too much and this defeats the conventional wisdom about performance peaking.

Time specific. When do you wish to reach your goal(s)? Short term goals may focus on the next few races or weeks of your programme. Longer term goals will likely deal with the next few seasons, where would you like to be 3—5 years from now?

In writing. Committing a goal to words adds a contractual component to your planning. It can serve as a gentle / or brutal reminder of the direction you have decided to go. I knew of a runner who painted his goals on his bedroom ceiling. If he didn't feel like running early in the morning he would just stare at his ceiling for a less than subtle reminder of his obligation to himself.

Ownership of goals is important. These are your goals, nobody else's. They are what you believe will help you become a better runner. Sharing these goals is also important for it allows you to form a mental contract with yourself; "*now that other people know my goals, I am going to have to do my best to reach them.*"

Never give up. How did you decide upon your goal? Running to success can be a solitary path sometimes. For a few runners that path seems paved with gold and there is nothing that can stop them. For us other mere mortals the path can be strewn with obstacles: injuries, losses of form, staleness, and other personal demons that limit our performance. Chart a path around these obstacles and never give up!

Is it time to reconsider your goals? If so, which "film" do you plan to make. Hopefully not a horror story or a farce! Why not make it an ACTION packed film. Enjoy your creation—it's what you've made it!

Shut off the lights!
Stop the cameras!
That's a wrap!

In a world where people will often say "that can't be done," somebody comes along, without inhibition and full of confidence. These people achieve the impossible and are responsible for a paradigm shift. Whether they are great scientists or explorers, athletes or humanitarians, they understand only too well that their talent, self-belief and the un-yielding pursuit of their dream is what will separate them from the rest.

The story of the first four minute mile is a tale that transcends running. It is a story of a man breaking down a barrier and exploring the range of human athletic potential.

The First Sub Four Minute Mile

The commemorative plaque at Iffley Road Stadium, Oxford, England is small and unassuming. The letters carefully carved onto its marble surface are clean and simple. With elegant understatement this plaque—fastened to the wall at the top of the spectator stand—gazes down on the running track and asks us to remember a race held on a blustery day in May, 1954…

Great Britain in the late 1940's was a place struggling with a persistent depression. The end of the 2nd World War had brought a short lived euphoria, but as the nation realised that the economic and social healing (let alone human healing) would take many years, a fugue fell over the country. In the early 1950's, however, there was a spirit of optimism sweeping the land. Queen Elizabeth II was coronated, Mount Everest was conquered, and the beloved Winston Churchill had returned from a brief political exile. It was hoped that this optimism would effectively counter balance the uncertainties posed by the dismantling of the British Empire.

Bursting into the nation's awareness were three young runners: Roger Bannister, a promising young miler, Christopher Chataway, an excellent distance runner, and Christopher Brasher—a young man with his sights firmly set on Olympic glory in the steeplechase event. The three runners attended Oxford University and quickly became friends. They were bright, erudite and each possessed a sense of purpose that they believed would propel them to remarkable achievements. They had powerful goals: Olympic medals, record times, but equally, if not more important, each young man was dedicated to the pursuit of a life of contribution and service. Bannister was to commit himself to medicine,

Chataway a career in politics and charitable projects, and Brasher was to become a successful business man and the director of the London Marathon.

The desire to be first has been a powerful driving force for many-a-athlete; and in 1954 Bannister found himself compelled to focus such energy and chase a unique opportunity in the history of running. The world record for the mile had steadily dropped over the previous decade and stood at 4minutes 1.4 seconds. Bannister fortuitously found himself rising to prominence as athletes all over the world raced to be the first human to run under four minutes for one mile. Winning a mile race in less than four minutes is one thing, but being the first ever was both a place in the record books and a special place in sporting history.

A race can be truly exciting if there is a strong possibility of defeat and Bannister faced many challengers in his quest. The American Wes Santee was setting the tracks on fire with some devastating front running while John Landy, the Australian, threatened to break the record in every race.

Bannister realized that a more scientific approach to his training would be needed if he was to break the record. With his coach, the legendary Franz Stampfl—Bannister referred to his medical knowledge of human physiology to bring fresh approaches to interval training, endurance recovery, and pacing. His preparations went well but balancing the demands of medical school and athletics was challenging. As the race approached, Bannister found himself tired and stale; qualities hardly conducive for writing your name into athletic history. Packing their ropes and climbing gear, Bannister and Brasher headed to Wales and vigorously ascended mountains for several days. Their spirits were rejuvenated and these "Miling Musketeers" (as they were called in the press) returned to Oxford with a renewed passion and urgency for the challenge before them.

Roger Bannister, Chris Chataway and Chris Brasher: Great friends, great runners!

The annual match between the Amateur Athletic Association and Oxford University was to be their chance, however, the weather conditions on May 6th, 1954 could not have been worse. A howling gale blew stinging cinders into the faces of athletes jogging around the track. Fast times seemed to be impossible. Bannister spent the day agonising over one key question: if he postponed this attempt would another runner (somebody like Landy) beat him to the record? Sometimes great moments are borne out of serendipity; as Bannister looked out of the window from his hotel room he noticed that the flags hanging stiffly from the flag poles momentarily sagged, the decision was made: "the attempt was on."

Three thousand spectators packed the stadium and there was a sense that something special was about to occur. It's not hard to imagine John Landy sitting by a radio waiting for news; the question *"would Bannister do it?"* undoubtedly sending adrenaline fizzing through his body.

Breaking the record required laps of 60 seconds or faster and it fell to Brasher to set the pace. Brasher might not have possessed the raw speed of Bannister, but he did possess the metronomic skills of an athlete who knows how to set a good pace. The first lap was reached in 57.5 seconds and Bannister, full of running, urged his friend to run even faster. Brasher ignored the request, thus preserving hopes of cracking the record. The half mile was reached in 1:58. Chataway, sensing that Brasher was starting to tire charged into the lead. Bannister followed lock and step. The sonorous clicks of the timekeeper's stopwatch were lost in the roar of the crowd; for some observers time moved faster, for Bannister it seemed agonizingly slow. With 300 yards left Bannister surged by Chataway, his final charge towards athletic destiny had begun.

"My body had long since exhausted all its energy, but I went on running just the same. The physical overdraft only came from greater willpower. This was the crucial moment when my legs were strong enough to carry me over the last few yards…with 5 yards to go the finishing tape seemed to recede. Would I ever reach it?…I leapt at the tape like a man taking his last spring to save himself from the chasm that threatens to engulf him." Had he done it? *" The stopwatch held the answer. Result of the one mile…time, 3minutes, the rest was lost in the roar of excitement. I grabbed Brasher and Chataway and scampered around the track in a burst of spontaneous joy. We had done—the three of us!"*

So why do we place so much interest on this world record, 3 minutes 59.4seconds? It only lasted 46 days, yet Sebastian Coe's World 800m record which lasted 16 years (it is still the second fastest ever) is seldom talked about. Perhaps it is our fascination with pioneers, people who have been the first to conquer a seemingly insurmountable challenge. Whether it was Sir Francis Chichester sailing single handed around the world (1966); Sir Edmund Hilary hiking towards the summit of Mount Everest (1953) or Neil Armstrong (1969) walking on the Moon, we are attracted to stories about people who change our perception of what is attainable.

Prior to Roger Bannister's run, the generally accepted belief was that no man could ever break a four minute mile. Now, such is athletic progress, we are disappointed if the race fails to yield such a time. Fifty years later the record has improved to an amazing 3minutes 43.13 seconds by Morroco's Hicham El

Guerrouj!

A poet once wrote "*even the stone that is kicked shall outlast Shakespeare.*" Great running careers will amaze us, mile records will be broken, but the stone plaque that hangs in a small stadium in Oxford shall outlast them all.

O.U.A.C.

On this track on May 6th 1954
ROGER GILBERT BANNISTER
Exeter College
President O.U.A.C. 1948-1949
ran one mile
in 3 minutes 59.4 seconds
*Thus becoming the first man to run
one mile in less than four minutes.*

Understanding Motivation and Running

The alarm went off at 5:25 a.m. John Smith—a half-decent marathon runner—rubbed the sleep from his face and pushed himself out of bed. Before starting yet another day at the office there was a training run to be completed. He checked his schedule: 5 miles steady with an emphasis on a gentle, relaxed rhythm. Smith laced up his trainers and headed out. Today he would run through the village before heading out onto the moors. Although his body initially ached he quickly found his pace. The cool morning air helped to sharpen his senses. He enjoyed the sight of heather starting to bloom. He felt the gentle crunch of an early morning frost under every step. The spells and spirits of Spring were hinting that the seasons were about to change. As the sun started to pour its golden rays over the moors, Smith felt completely alive and full of running; "*it doesn't get any better than this,*" he whispered between breaths.

On the other side of town Billy Matthews ignored the jarring tones of his alarm clock. "*Just a few more minutes sleep,*" he scowled. 30 minutes later that was a rap on the door "*Billy, get-up, we've got to get going.*" Several of Billy's teammates had arrived to drag him out for that early morning run. Billy begrudgingly hauled himself out of bed and joined his friends. The cold air did nothing to lighten his temper. 40 minutes later, the run was over. "*That was no fun, it's too cold and too early*" Billy snapped at his friends. "*Remember, Billy, you're doing this to help us win that relay race, nobody said that you have to enjoy it,*" they replied. Billy nodded his head in agreement before returning to his sullen mood.

Why is it that on some days we are a "John Smith" relishing the sensations of a run in nature? Other days we can be like Billy Matthews, slogging through the routine of an early morning run to "get the job done."

Attempts to understand motivation has challenged some of the world's greatest psychologists. From Freud (with his pleasure-pain principle) to Maslow (with his hierarchy of needs theory), psychologists from many schools of thought have pitched their explanations for human behaviour.

Undoubtedly human beings are complex creatures and runners are probably amongst the most complicated! There is something unique in the soul of the runner that drives us to run in torrential rain, take pleasure in popping a well earned blister, or continuing to race to the line when defeat is but a certainty. A famous cognitive psychologist, Niesser, once stated *"no system can ever truly understand itself,"* this begs the question: is there any point then in analysing our motives for running, especially since our reasons might change from one day to the next? Aristotle the great Greek philosopher might have countered *"the unexamined life is not worth living."* This might be a bit heavy-handed but it can be argued that a clear understanding of your reasons for running will help you to avoid burn-out and disappointment.

While an athlete's motives for running are many, they are undoubtedly shaped by powerful forces in the world in which we run. Let's examine two of these "forces": culture and environment.

Some cultures have such a reverence for running that it inspires runners to reach the very highest levels of achievement. England in the 1980's was such a place creating legions of world record holders: Coe, Ovett, Cram, Elliot, Moorcroft, Steve Jones. Their successes inspired tens of thousands of runners to take to the streets and try their hand at this most noble of sports.

- When people around you are being successful it creates a buzz, an excitement, that helps to motivate other runners to train and race hard. Seek out that environment and allow yourself to be inspired.

Running is also one of the most natural of sports. A primary means of transportation in our evolution, running presents a way for us to spiritually and emotionally connect with the world around us. For many athletes, running on the moors is infinitely preferable to running in the city—but such is the capricious nature of a human that even that cannot be said to hold true for all runners.

- Find ways to run in the environment that brings you the greatest pleasure and a sense of release from the stresses of daily life.

Sports psychologists have described athletes that have a strong internal drive (such as "John Smith"), i.e. they run for personal, introspective reasons, as being intrinsically motivated. Runners who train or compete for rewards or satisfaction from external sources are said to be extrinsically motivated. These broad categories are a bit simplistic and fail to identify the vast range of motives that shape an athlete's performance and enjoyment of running.

Alfred Adler, one of the most famous psychologists from the early 20th century suggested that people strive to improve themselves, in-part because they want to overcome feelings of inferiority, and also because this will help them to develop and grow. Adler listed a number of motives (highlighted below) that can be influential in our lives:

Power / mastery—some people are motivated to run because this gives them a sense of mastery over their body, perhaps a sense of accomplishment. Achieving this state can also create power and in some cases a feeling of superiority over another runner with whom you are competing against.

The need for achievement (sometimes called n'ach) was recognised by the psychologist McClelland as a significant determinant of success in sports performance. Athletes with a high need to achieve are characterised by having a competitive streak matched with a determination to reach a goal. These athletes are frustrated with anything less than total success (whatever that personally means for them). The pursuit of excellence, the demonstration to others of a high level of skill (exhibition), and sometimes aggressive behaviour on the sports field also define these athletes.

Athletes with a low need for achievement are probably quite content to run in the pack and take whatever results come their way. Such runners are probably more motivated by a need for body sentience i.e. they run because they like the connection with nature. Affiliation with teammates is also a prime motive. Other motives that describe this runner include sensation—they enjoy the feelings associated with running hard. Running for this athlete is just another form of play; it is something that has to be fun or it is not worth doing.

- How would you describe yourself? Do you have a high or low n'ach? Which motive for participation is the most important to you? Have you lost sight of why you run? Take a moment to reflect on these questions…

There are other theories that can explain running behaviour. The deficiency motivation theory describes a runner that is seeking to restore their physical or psychological equilibrium. Athletes who are recovering—either from injury or setback are likely using this need to speed their return to form.

Growth motivation theory implies that some runners may wish to go to a new level of performance; it is this desire for betterment that throws them out onto the training road in all weather.

Not all theories are considered positive motives for participation, however. Fear of failure can motivate some athletes to extraordinary levels of performance. However, when a setback occurs, these athletes may experience difficulty in coping with their feelings.

Sometimes we need a gentle reminder to bring balance and perspective to our training and racing. Reaching a clearer understanding of your motivation for running might help you to achieve this balance.

"It's a con game!"—Confidence and running

The Sydney Olympic Games marathon was about to begin and the tension and excitement was almost palpable. Razor-thin athletes stared out toward that famous harbour believing or hoping that it would be their athletic destiny to claim victory. For those of us watching the final race preparations unfold it was apparent that several athletes were seeking to gain an edge, some sort of advantage over their rivals even before the race started. Some athletes growled about the warm-up area eager to slap down a rival with a vicious scowl. A few were more subtle; a smirk, perhaps a reductive remark. The body language of several World Champions was suggestive of a gauntlet: "*You haven't got what it takes!*" While a few athletes were poker-faced neither wishing to display bravado nor mask insecurity—"*I am going to keep everyone guessing about me throughout the race.*" It is interesting to compare these various styles with the actual results: Jon Brown of England wearing a look of determination, a man preparing to spring a surprise. The Kenyans and Ethiopeans: A quiet but intense confidence preparing to infuse their strides.

To compete at a successful level athletes know that they must bring many elements of their training into sharp focus on race day. The hard workouts have been replaced by a taper, then rest. Careful thought has been given to pre-race meals and early nights in bed are planned. The execution of this performance is, however, heavily dependent on the athlete's level of confidence. Confidence is both a belief system and a way of carrying yourself; but confidence wears many masks and is not always easy to understand. It can be imperious at its celebratory best, modest in words before and after an event, and yet arrogant in its actions. Confidence for some athletes can also be difficult to acquire and yet easy to lose. The belief in yourself may also vary across the race; for instance you could be calm at the start, edgy in the middle of the race and a nervous wreck at the finish. So how do you develop confidence given its ever-changing qualities and become a better athlete?

Firstly, recognise that part of confidence is a mental skill that can be trained with the same principles of physical training. Do you practise building your confidence on a regular basis or do you hope that it will occur by chance? Why leave such an important part of your preparation to serendipity? A positive outlook on life in general is a good starting point but that in itself is not necessarily going to benefit your training and racing. Two techniques from sports psychology have been proven to be effective when practised on a regular basis: Mental rehearsal and affirmation training.

Mental rehearsal is where the athlete thinks about their ideal performance over and over in their mind. Like an actor rehearsing your lines, eventually, you will not need to "think" about being confident your performance, it becomes so ingrained into your thinking that it is almost automatic. Athletics using this technique could rehearse their race tactics. They may "see" themselves surging on a difficult part of the course. They might mentally practise fending off a challenge from determined rivals. If athletes have a confidence issue with part of their race, they might try playing that image in their mind and seeing themselves confidently conquering their fear. They could practise thinking about how their bodies will respond and they will "see" themselves competing with every step and stroke being powerful, controlled, and full of self-belief. It is important to practise the things that you can control; i.e. your effort and your technique. The results take care of themselves.

Positive statements, affirmations as they are called in sports psychology, will reinforce the aspects of your training (or racing) that went well. *"Don't beat yourself up—build yourself up!" "As you believe so you will become!"*
Evidence suggests that practising such statements combined with mental rehearsal training are useful tools in building an athlete's confidence. There are also some practical ways to give shape your mental training:

- Set yourself workouts where you know there will be a high chance of being successful. You may have to modify the workout, e.g. make the time trial over a shorter distance than race distance.

- Train with other athletes that will help to give you a positive benchmark of your level of fitness. Again, choose those that will give you a boost, not bury you on the road!

Remember that confidence contributes to success and this, in turn, enhances confidence. How you choose to display confidence is up to you. It is easy to step back and be critical of the more vocal athletes whom rely on bold statements to create their self-belief. Ultimately, they are no different from the silent gaze of the quiet athlete who is determined to kick your hide into last week. Choose your style, mentally rehearse and have the belief that it is going to work for you!

A heroic performance is within you!

The Spartans, who were not only fearsome warriors but also dedicated participants at the ancient Olympic Games, were often sent into battle with the rallying cry to either come home on a shield (i.e. dead!) or with a shield in their hand. Life for these ancient Greeks contained two defining themes, heroism and tragedy. Great feats of heroism were expected in battle, but to die in fear was viewed as tragic. The Greeks weaved these threads into their dramas, they became the key elements of their storytelling; and fittingly, as the latest Olympic flame has just been extinguished, they were also found in sporting contests.

The champions at this year's Olympic Games, once again, celebrated the diversity of the athletic gene pool. They ran with many styles and for many reasons. They delivered feats of athletic heroism and yet many personally understood only too well the tragic surprises that sometimes emerge from sport.

There was diminutive Ethiopean, Kenese Bekele, conquering the 10km with flowing strides; a withering 53 second last lap to leave his rivals pondering the thought *"what does it take to beat this man?"* The Russian, Yuri Borzakovskiy, was all muscle and power, his timing and delivery over the 800m was impeccable. A different kind of runner was Kelly Holmes, a ferocious study of intense concentration; a runner secure with the confidence that she is in the shape of her life. Then there was the mesmerising rythms of Hicham El Guerrouj, winner of the 1500m and 5000m; a runner whose lengthy stride elegantly contrasted the staccato steps of Mizuko Noguchi, the women's marathon champion.

Fitness and technique can explain much of the success of these wonderful athletes, but a study of some of these runners will likely tell a story that is in stark contrast to the celebrity that accompanies the heights of athletic achievement. It will not be uncommon to hear tales of deprivation and poverty, injury and illness. The pages of their biographies will be scarred by a lack of opportunity or marred by setback. And yet, despite hardships they have succeeded.

A case-in-point is the story of Hicham El Guerrouj. Despite numerous world records, he had never won an Olympic title. At the Atlanta Olympic Games El Guerrouj was the clear favorite but was (tragically?) tripped early in the race. He failed to finish. Four years later in Sydney he was defeated by the narrowest of margins. Would he stare down setback and adversity and finally claim an Olympic title? As El Guerrouj battled the Kenyan—Bernard Legat—to the line, some commentators suggested that it appeared that El Guerrouj *"just wanted it more."* He claimed his gold!

Does desire, and by extension athletic success, have to be born out of hardship? The virtues of "the school of hard knocks" are often estolled by poets and philosophers: *"Suffering is the only true source of conciousness"* –said Dostoyevsky; *"Success is going from failure to failure without losing your enthusiasm,"* said Winston Churchill. But these somewhat grim appraisals would suggest that fun and enjoyment are not necessary qualities for an athlete to achieve greatness. Is this true?

There is an old adage in sport that *"the difference between the ordinary and extraordinary is the little extra."* What is the "extra" that separates the good from the great? Does it lie in the psychological make-up of the athlete?

The psychological characteristics of great runners

Sports psychology has—for decades—attempted to identify any qualities that specifically define a champion athlete. Not surprisingly, given the complexity of humans—the questionnaires that were developed were not reliable in identifying stable traits in a personality that "created" the champion athlete.

Research has increasingly focused on what is known as the "states" of a champion athlete's mental condition. Two psychologists, Williams and Krane, identified a cluster of skills that would seem to separate athletes. High levels of motivation and a passionate commitment to excellence featured significantly in high achieving athletes—no surprises there. The ability to concentrate, set goals, regulate levels of arousal were also identified as important skills. A carefully defined competitive plan, a pre-race routine that enhanced the athlete's state of mental preparation, were also critical.

What is apparent here is that all of these skills can be learned. Techniques to enhance motivation, strategies to sharpen concentration, breathing skills to control levels of arousal can be applied by any athlete with the will to develop their mental skills. Highly successful athletes have incorporated these practises into their training and racing so that it is almost an involuntary action—i.e. it is something that they draw upon almost without thinking about it.

New ideas are emerging that suggest "adaptive perfectionism" and high degrees of optimism are qualities that champion athletes thrive upon. But what if you don't exhibit some of these behaviours, or you find that this concentrated approach takes away from the simple pleasures of running; are you consigned to the ranks of the "also-rans?" A few years ago I was chatting with a Kenyan runner—Daniel Komen—who was tearing up the record books with his brilliant running. I asked him what psychological techniques he used to help him concentrate. He looked bemused, shrugged his shoulders and said, "I just run."

Just as the Spartans marched into battle expecting to perform heroic deeds, you too should enter races expecting to achieve your very best. It is this belief (and the skills that can be used to enhance it) that separate the good from the great.

Risk-taking and running
Is it all in the run of the dice?

After a recent trip to Las Vegas I reflected on the sound of coins being tossed into slot machines as if they were electronic wishing wells. There were those images of the cards crisply falling onto baize and the nerve jangling uncertainty from the spin of the roulette wheel. I was reminded of the gambles that runners take in their training and racing.

In gambling parlance, the player needs to calculate the odds and see if they can "beat the house." The strategies used by runners in a race is no different. All runners need to assess their opponents, decide their best tactic for success, maybe put on a "poker-face" and prepare to call the bluff of an equally determined rival.

The thrill of a gamble carries the possibilities of rich rewards, but equally the chance of defeat or setback (the latter of which is quite likely if you're in Vegas!). A runner can choose tactics that "play it safe" and stay within their usual range of achievement, or they can take risks, try something different and explore their untapped veins of performance.

Some runners are natural risk-takers. They will surge to the front of the field with an unexpected tactic and wreak havoc on the pacing strategies of other runners. These athletes thrive on the thrill of running at the edge, they keep us all guessing (and themselves) to see if they can maintain that pace to the finish. There are also those runners who throw all caution away realising there is probably no chance for success but in the spirit of "give it a go" they race anyway.

For elite athletes like Paula Radcliffe, risk-taking is a well-defined skill, but unlike us "mortal athletes" she backs up her strategies with a supreme level of fitness that actually minimises the odds of defeat. For her the risk of a setback comes from not carrying out her plan.

While Buddha might cringe at the thought of being connected to an article on gambling and risk taking, a few of his words are particularly salient:

"Deeds can become habits, habits can become character." The habits of risk-taking running—with all its intrinsic rewards—could become ingrained in the athletes racing personality if success is achieved. Drawing on the classic principles of behavioral psychology, an athlete that achieves success from a risky strategy is more likely to attempt similar behaviour next time out; i.e. the behaviour is reinforced. Thus, it is particularly important to set goals that give you a realistic chance of success rather than forming a pattern of continual disappointment. Runners who drop out of races increase the likelihood that they will drop out of future races if things become tough.

Runners that demonstrate a strong risk-taking profile tend to exhibit similar mental skills:

- Confidence—to apply a race plan even though it may carry the strong chance for setback
- Courage—to see the plan through to its conclusion and the willingness to accept the outcome
- Determination to execute carefully designed tactics

How do you become a risk-taking runner?

- Set goals that will take your training and racing to a level where you have never been before. The practise of repeatedly trying new techniques and strategies will eventually become a habit.

- Balance risk and realism—There are good risks—a goal that focuses on beating a rival that matches your own talent level, and foolish risks—trying to beat the world record holder when you are still a club level athlete. By all means, aim high, but setting unrealistic goals is not risk-taking running, it is certain defeat and can undermine your confidence.

- Try a new tactic. Experiment in training with a strategy that tests your limits. There will be doubts in your mind that you can sustain this strategy, but try to talk yourself through these and believe that this goal is attainable. Once again, this will become a habit and will seem like second nature when the chance to apply it in a race arrives.

- Race an unfamiliar distance and praise your efforts for trying something different.

- Don't allow the stopwatch to tell you if you have been successful. Gauge your success on the effort that you have made.

- Remember...*and now for the cliches....Nothing ventured, nothing gained! No guts, no glory!*

Running races can often be gamble, sometimes you just have to roll the dice and see what happens. Good luck!

How to beat the unbeatable runner!

There are many types of runners: there are the talented and the determined; there are the courageous and the plain crazy. But there is a certain type of runner that we all secretly admire and maybe a part of us also wants to hate. This is the athlete that appears at the top of the results sheets of every age-group race; they are highly respected and widely known as "the unbeatable athlete." Race in, race out, this runner always seems to have an edge over us. They are either that much fitter or just seem to make the right tactical moves at the right time. No matter how hard we try, they just seem to have our number. Once you get past the frustration of being beaten by this athlete, may be you should consider the following question:

Who is the unbeatable runner and how can I beat him?

The profile of this seemingly invincible athlete initially makes for some unsettling reading. This runner is supremely confident and fully in control of all aspects of their performance. They seem to glide through the air as if they have invisible wings on their feet. Their technique seems so perfect that it appears to mock the rest of us shuffling hard across the ground in search of respectability. There can be a ruthless edge to their racing, some just want to win with style, a few (more maniacal) want to tear you apart. When they race there is an inherent confidence—if not arrogance—infusing every step that they take. An excellent performance, in their mind, is a certainty.

These "unbeatable" athletes have either earned or created a reputation that precedes them, and sometimes too much respect is afforded them in a race. The great Steve Ovett once stated that he had won many races by reputation alone. He was having a bad day and should have been beaten, however, his opponents lacked the self-belief that this great athlete could be defeated. Athletes—such as Ovett—then manage to string together a lengthy undefeated streak. This reinforces the mystique and sentiment that this athlete is "unbeatable." One day, a runner comes along and springs a shock surprise, the un-thinkable happens, our hero is beaten. Other athletes sensing the weakening of this runner then line up to "have a go."

- Plan to defeat him; you have to start with the belief that that day will surely come. The belief system that states that this runner cannot be defeated can easily turn into a self-fulfilling prophecy for some runners. Rather than waiting for somebody else to come along and shatter that belief, why can't it be you?

- Accept the notion that reaching the top is tough, but staying there is even tougher. This unbeatable athlete has the knowledge that there is no allowance for a bad day. Everyone is out to get them. No matter how good you are, somebody wants to take your place at the top. This insidious thought is the Achilles heel of this great athlete. They know that sooner or later they will meet their match and this thought can have a corrosive effect on their confidence.

- Like a punter at the horse races you should be a keen study of the form. Has your unbeatable athlete been racing too much? Are they suspect over certain distances? Do they use the same winning tactics in each race? Have they made any mistakes in their racing strategy that you could exploit? Try to anticipate when they might have a bad day. Do they have to travel a long way for the race? Have they recently been ill? Do they seem to be struggling in their warm-up? With careful consideration of these points you can formulate a plan that might just spring that surprise.

- Deliver the tactical plan with courage and assertion. An "unbeatable athlete" has achieved their success by knowing how to read the tactics of others and counter them with a plan of their own. If your tactical move is not decisive they will believe that it is a weakly disguised bluff. When you make your move in a race, do so forcefully, no half-measures. Run with the commitment to break away from this runner.

- Test your rival's fitness with several probing surges. These are accelerations for short distances that attempt to measure your rival's response. You may steal a few yards, if they seem to be struggling maintain the surge for a few more metres then relax. You should gain confidence that your rival has been caught off guard.

Racing that unbeatable athlete is never going to be easy. They have earned that moniker; no-one has given it to them. However, perhaps you should comfort yourself with the thought that throughout history all empires—no matter how dominant—have eventually fallen.

Maybe you never beat your nemesis, but there is an old adage in running "if you can't beat the fellow in front of you, make sure that he breaks the record!"

Facing a tough rival is a given when you participate in running races. Everyone has their nemesis. Perhaps it is an age-group rival that you have battled for years, or maybe it is a friend in high school that you want to beat. No matter how good you are there is always somebody who wants to take your place at the front. Confidence has always been a critical part of a successful runner's make-up, but it is easy to be confident when things are going your way. A greater test of confidence is when there is threat and the strong possibility of defeat in front of you. How then, do you respond? In 1954, only two runners had broken the 4 minute mile, Roger Bannister and John Landy. Both were mercurial talents. Each had the confidence to win. Sporting destiny drew them together in a test of fitness and confidence. One was confident that front running would win the race, one was confident that waiting and sprinting would clinch victory. Who would win? Sit back and enjoy…

The Miracle Mile

They called it **"*The Miracle Mile*"** and for good reason. In August, 1954, only two runners in the history of distance running had broken the four minute mile—Roger Bannister from England and John Landy from Australia. They were the talk of the globe; two runners shattering records and leading humanity into uncharted regions of athletic potential. It seemed only natural that sporting destiny should demand that they should be brought together to race. The public had many questions that needed an answer: Landy had been beaten by Bannister to the first sub 4 minute mile by just 46 days; his place in history denied: Was Landy out for revenge?

Bannister had proven himself to be adept at chasing records, but how would he fair against such a fearless competitor and dazzling frontrunner as John Landy?

It was almost prophetic when Bannister said, *"the mile has all the elements of a drama."* "The "Miracle Mile" promised to be a race of epic proportions.

As the race approached, the opinions of the sporting public started to take shape. We generally love sharp contrasts in our sporting rivalries: the arrogant athlete versus the modest; the overwhelming favourite versus the underdog. With Bannister and Landy the contrasts were difficult to identify. Both were polite and unassuming; each athlete had a deep and genuine respect for one another. When asked how he felt when Bannister broke the record Landy replied *"I wasn't disappointed but amazed.*" The bookmakers made Landy a 4:1 favourite based on the fact that he had reduced Bannister's record from 3mins.59.6secs to a stunning 3mins.57.9 secs. But everybody knew there was very little that would separate these great athletes come race day.

Today, it seems we want our sporting heroes to have a touch of pirate blood coarsing through their veins: a ruthless instinct to plunder victory if there is so much as a whiff of success to be had in a race. While the piratical motives were present in both athletes, they also exhibited a profound appreciation for the joy of movement. They viewed a favourable outcome of a race to be desirable but of greater value was the opportunity to measure their talent and fitness against the World's best. This was sporting competition distilled to its very essence: A man against another: A man against himself!

In August, 1954 the British Empire was celebrating its very last sporting festival, The Empire Games, although they were to be re-invented four years later as The Commonwealth Games. The magnificent city of Vancouver, British Columbia, Canada played host and more spectacular site for "The Miracle Mile" could not have been found.

The games were held in Empire Stadium, a small wooden facility with clean and simple lines of architecture that did not minimise the performances on its track. The snow capped Coastal Mountains served as a powerful back drop; these sparkling peaks stared directly into the stadium and reminded us that nature and pure sporting performance are kindred spirits. Pacific breezes should have cooled the summer air, but on that day they were absent. The temperature on the track soared, the eyes of the World watched and in this crucible two of the greatest athletes prepared to bare their sporting souls for examination.

The starter's commands brought the competitors to the line.

Landy took his position, his shuffling stutter-steps reminiscent of a sail cutting across the choppy waters of Sydney Harbour. Curiously, a runner next to Landy adopted a sprint start, what were his intentions for the race? Roger Bannister eased forward looking relaxed and confident. It almost seems strange that an experience of a lifetime (for athletes and spectators) can be condensed into just four minutes. Years of hard training, weeks of speculation had come to this… the gun released the runners and the crowd immediately knew that something special was underway.

There was some speculation in the press that the race might be anti-climatic, two brilliant runners nervously sparring, too frightened to lose that they fail to unleash their full potential. How wrong they were. After the initial gallop at the start, Landy took the lead and dispelled any notions of a tactical "cat and mouse" race. His pace was fast, powerful and carried the determination of man prepared to carry the challenge to his rival. Landy quickly established a lead that seemed to stretch with every stride. First it was 5 yards, then 10 yards, and by the half mile the lead had grown to 15 yards. Could Bannister recover such a deficit? Would Landy be strong enough to hold the pace? Another sub four minute mile seemed inevitable, would the record be broken yet again?

Bannister must have felt like a shadowy, almost ghostly presence to Landy, he couldn't be seen but Landy knew he was there. Landy once said *"The mile has a classic symmetry…it's a play in four acts."* If the first two laps were just setting the scene, the next two were about to bring high drama! Moving towards the end of the 3rd lap, Bannister realised that he would need to move onto Landy's shoulder if he was to have any chance of unleashing his devastating sprint finish. Bannister later said *"I tried to imagine myself attached to him by some invisible cord. With each stride, I drew the cord tighter and reduced his lead."*

Into the final lap Landy still lead. He piled on the pace making his move for the finish from 300 yards out. Bannister, who had overextended himself just by closing gap, found that it was all he could do just to stay close. The crowd were almost hypnotised by these two great athletes who were battling the fatigue pinching their muscles; their minds refusing to yield. Onto the top bend they charged and Bannister then made his move. Mustering all his reserves, he flung himself toward Landy and then one of the great moments in sports history took place. Landy sensed that Bannister was close and mistakenly looked over his left shoulder to see where his rival was. At that very moment, Bannister surged past on Landy's right shoulder. Bannister was in-front and raced on to victory with Landy in valiant pursuit.

The Miracle Mile had delivered. Both runners ran under the four minutes (Bannister 3mins 58.8 secs, Landy 3mins 59.6 secs) but were just outside Landy's world record. After the race, Bannister saluted his magnanimous rival: *"John Landy has shown me what a race can really be at its greatest. He is the sort of runner that I could never become, and for this I admire him."*

Today, there is nothing left of the old Empire Stadium, the track and its memories long surrendered to property development. However, a bronze statue of two great runners can still be found; one runner looking over his left shoulder, the other preparing to pass. It will remind you that miracles do come true.

"Tune in" to a better running performance

Another race has been decided and the winners have practically galloped across the finishing line; the envy of many-an-athlete. While other athletes stagger to the line like drunken metronomes, this rare species of humanity is busy collecting their accolades. These are the athletes who can churn out miles on the road with the efficiency of a well-oiled machine. They can flow across the pavement apparently oblivious to their fatigue. And yet, they are the one's who endure the discomforts of a hard race for the least amount of time! 2/3hours of hard racing is tough, but isn't 4/5 hours tougher? These athletes—the ones that you will find on the 18th page of the results sheets—are the ghostly spirits of the sport; their presence is felt but not always seen. They are the athletes that fade away from the finishing line to have their blisters popped by a loved one—not an athletic trainer with an alphabet of qualifications after their name.

Throughout the long hours out on the course well-meaning spectators will be offering a plethora of cliches to help these weary athletes through their fatigue. The origins of these cliches vary: there is the bar-room inspired "suck it up, buddy!" There is the sports psychologist's couch "keep your focus!" And of course, the locker room "when the going gets tough…" Does any of this advice really help? 4 hours is a long time to "focusing," and it's definitely a long time to be "sucking" (I guess you could interpret that one in several ways!)

Sustained concentration is difficult, especially when your body is pouring fatigue into every sinew. As the mind wanders, thoughts of despair polluting the possibility of a great performance, it is not surprising that an athlete can miss their predicted times by many minutes, if not hours. Is there any way that an athlete can use their mental skills to improve performance, to shove aside these demons and let all their hard training bring the rewards that they deserve?

Two techniques from sports psychology offer fascinating possibilities.

Association is a mental technique that requires the endurance athlete to concentrate on many aspects of their physical condition. The athlete repeatedly runs through a mental checklist of body signals ensuring that everything is operating in a range that will allow the athlete to complete the race at top speed.

For example, the athlete might ask themselves the following questions: Is my breathing relaxed? Is this a pace that I can hold for the rest of the race? Are my muscles coping? Is there any sign of cramping? Can I increase the pace? Etc.

The athlete concentrates on these physical signals and responds with either a tactical adjustment (slowing down, speeding up, surging, etc). The purpose of this technique is to help keep fatigue at the greatest intensity the athlete can cope with before there is a decrease in performance. Research suggests that this technique is most effective for elite athletes.

Dissociation is a technique that trains the athlete to block thoughts of fatigue. The athlete is encouraged to think about anything…play their favorite cd in their mind, recite their favorite poems, recall fun times…that will distract them. Several studies have shown that novice athletes who use dissociation strategies improve their times much more than athletes (doing the same physical training program) who primarily use association strategies.

Tests with athletes that have been trained to use the dissociation technique have found that their perception of exertion was manipulated; they learned to ignore their fatigue. This may be advantageous in competitions but it is not without its risks. There have been cases where athletes suffered serious dehydration because they failed to recognise their bodies' signals of distress. Dissociation may also reduce the athlete's ability to make rapid decisions in response to race tactics. Athletes becoming too absorbed in their thoughts may start to lose their sense of pace judgement and find that they have been slowing down without realising it. Another study has suggested that dissociation may contribute to an athlete "hitting the wall" the reasoning being that the athlete ignored the physical signals that indicated they were running too fast.

Summary

A combination of both techniques is probably the most effective. Try this strategy next time you race: "Tune in" to your physical signals by monitoring your breathing, learn to relax when tense, relieve muscle tension by adjusting your pace, read your energy levels—be honest in your assessment—can you really keep this up? If all is well then "tune out."

Running in the zone

Anyone with an appreciation for the history of British distance running will almost certainly look back at the 1980's as one of those truly golden eras in our sport. It was a time when "Brittania ruled…the track," with British athletes holding the world records for 800m, 1000m, 1500m, mile, 5000, and the marathon. We all have our favorite memories: perhaps it was Coe versus Ovett at the Moscow 1500m, or Cram destroying the field to win the world 1500m championships, or Steve Jones pulling away from Charlie Spedding to win the London Marathon.

The performances were remarkable, but I think what particularly caught the publics imagination was the supreme ease with which these athletes ran. While other athletes were straining to squeeze every ounce of effort from their talent, our runners seemed to apply grace, style, and relaxed speed in ways that could devastate a field. They almost seemed to defy the accepted wisdom that you are at your most tired at the end of the race; the sprinting kicks of Coe and Ovett off very fast paces humbled other world class athletes.

And yet, there is also an accepted truth in history, that all empires eventually crumble and the British distance running hegemony proved no different. As our leading athletes aged a surprise defeat here, an injury there, and before we wanted to accept it, that era had passed.

In studying many of these great athletes and their stellar performances a number of recurring themes emerged: Each runner could give a seemingly effortless performance. They were fearless about failure, exhibited heightened confidence and optimism, and had boundless energy. At the peak of their careers, these amazing athletes could be said to have been "running in the zone."

What is the zone?

In the 1970's a Hungarian psychologist named Csikszentmihalyi developed an idea known as Flow. He was interested in how creative people—artists, jazz players, pianists, and then athletes—reach heightened states of performance. He noted that people seem to enter a "flow state" when they are fully absorbed in activity during which they lose their sense of time and have feelings of great satisfaction.

People who were in the flow state (or in the zone) reported that they felt an "ecstatic state." They were completely focused, concentrating on the task. They had a clear understanding of what needed to be done and how well they were doing with the task. They knew that their skills could match the challenge. They exhibited, and felt, a complete sense of calm and that they could control the race. There are also reports of athletes in a flow state not noticing the passing of time.

Csikszentmihalyi suggested that a major problem for many runners is that they have conscious of a fear of how they appear to others and what those people might think. Certainly athletes who are at a participation level and have sensitivity about their body image will have some difficulties achieving a flow state in running. For these runners to achieve this state, they would need to stop thinking / worrying what other people might be saying about them.

Although relaxation is a key feature of athletes "in the zone," this phenomenon seems to occur when the athlete is significantly challenged. A characteristic sign that the runner is about to enter a flow state is a narrowing of attention (concentration). They feel absorbed in the activity as if nothing else exists. They do not focus on the outcome—that looks after itself. Instead, they are supremely confident that they will deliver an excellent performance.

There is a cliché in sports psychology that suggests an athlete can sometimes fall prone to "analysis—paralysis"; an overemphasis on minor details while searching for performance enhancement. In the 1980's the book "The Inner Game of Tennis" by Tim Gallaway suggested ways of helping players make their strokes seem automatic. "The Inner Game" approach was to draw on influences of Zen philosophy: "*Great works are done when one is not calculating or thinking.*" (Suzuki—Zen Master).

How can we train ourselves to enter into a flow state?

- Flow occurs when the challenges are evenly matched with the athlete's skills. So to experience this phenomenon you will need to design your racing and your goals to have realistic expectations.

- Flow is born out of confidence and relaxation. These skills should be practised in training. Give yourself workouts that will bring repeated success. Train your muscles to move without tension and with efficiency.

- Try not to make it happen, just let it happen.

- Use affirmation statements. Key words to help you move toward this state include: automatic, unconcious effort, movement with out thought, flow across the track.

Use mental visualisation—Imagine yourself running in a flow state. See yourself moving effortlessly, in control and with complete concentration on your form. Practise this from an internal and external perspective. Imagine how it feels (internal) and what it looks like (external).

Running through the Looking Glass

The race is about to begin. The announcer introduces the star athletes and they wave to the appreciative crowd. You jog purposefully in the middle of the pack. The rabbit for the race does a few final strides; there is definitely a spring in his step. The rabbit takes a pocket watch out, looks at it and decides that it is time to start running. He beckons the runners to follow him…The runners obediently start to move forward, however a few metres into the run they suddenly fall into a hole that has opened in the ground in front of them…you close your eyes and start falling. When you open your eyes, you are again on a starting line. "Welcome to WonderLand" declares the rabbit. The next race is "The Lexicon of Running 10km"…"But I don't where I am going" you shout at the rabbit. *"Begin at the beginning, and go on till you come to the end. Then stop!"* he replies. Sounds simple enough.

The starting gun fires and runners, wearing words from the running dictionary on their chests, instead of numbers, stride into action. A runner wearing Aerobic sets off at a good clip; his mischievous twin, Anaerobic, impatiently follows to see if he makes a mess of the pace. You desperately try to match this cracking speed. You note the words on some of the runners that you are starting to pass: Fartlek, who has started to walk and Fun who doesn't seem to be taking things seriously. Lactate appears to be wobbling all over the course and Miles is definitely in for the long haul. You run by Physiology and Psychology who try to shout some advice at you: *"If you want to get somewhere you must run at least twice as fast as that."* You're not sure that that is helpful. On you continue. Obsession runs by and stares at you like a condemning mirror. You choose to ignore him. *"And thick and fast they came at last and more and more and more,"* until they reached the end.

Our modern world is a very demanding one. *"Now, now, cried the Queen, faster, faster!"* and it is a place where *"it takes all the running that you can do to keep in the same place!"* You understand this only too well. This is as fast as you can go; you are already working 12—14 hour days, may be raising a family, and if lucky enough to find some spare time, trying to excel at our sport. You would like to complain *"For some of us are out breath."* But who is listening? Do you feel like you are living in a Lewis Carroll fantasy world?

It would seem that the rabbit's timepiece is an apt metaphor for the pressing demands made on our lives. We wake, work and play according to the ticking of a clock. We allow it to tell us when we have relaxed enough or if we are in danger of missing a deadline. In our running lives we can let the watch be the judge of our performance; but it lacks a discriminating appreciation for our efforts. In its mind, you have either run fast or you haven't. It is blunt and meticulous and finds few friends amongst the fatigued.

A balanced existence is offered as a way of finding inner satisfaction and for runners, a path to better performances. Finding that equilibrium in life and love, work and play is easy to write about but seemingly difficult to incorporate into our urban existence. While the desire to play more and work less is fully understood by children, somehow when we become adults, we find ways to avoid the powerful drives of this innate need. Running (and play in general) is meant to be a source of stress release. It provides an opportunity to let the strain of work and other life challenges dissipate in the invigorating country air. Sadly, for an athlete that has become too competitive, obsessively focused on achievement and performance, it can quickly become an angst-filled distraction. Joy leaves those who do not lead balanced lives; for runners this especially holds true.

Studies have shown that high achieving athletes often perform better when they have other things in their lives other than running. Being a dedicated athlete, prepared to run in all weather and tolerate the discomforts of hard training doesn't make you a psychologically unhealthy individual. It is only when this occurs at the expense of the other components of life can this prove to be counter-productive.

I think we would all like to be like the Lewis Carroll character that *"went so fast that at last he seemed to skim through the air, hardly touching the ground with his feet."* Find the balance in your life and let the ground disappear beneath you!

The psychology of injuries

Two weeks before this year's London Marathon, Barry Tompkins knew that he was ready for a great run. Months of disciplined living, diligent training and a determination to *"get the job done,"* seemed like the essential ingredients for success. In his final long run, however, he noticed a tightness on the side of his quad that refused to ease no matter how much he adjusted his pace. A few days later the soreness had still not disappeared. Deciding that it was nothing more than a bit of muscular stiffness he went out for a brisk 10 mile run. Three miles into it that quiet nagging sensation became a loud and jarring throb. He was forced to stop and walk home. The diagnosis was severe inflammation of the Ilio-tibial band; it didn't really matter what it was, he was officially injured! He didn't make it to the start line.

What is the cause of injury?

Injuries seem to fall into two easily defined categories: those that occur by accident and those that result from overuse. Let's focus on the overuse for it is here that the runner is able to exert some control over proceedings. In most things in life, the more we practise the better we become. It is thus a cruel paradox of running that if you practise too much, you can become injured and have—potentially—nothing to show for all your hours of dedication, self-sacrifice and effort.

An overuse injury is essentially a failure to cope with the stress load that an athlete places on their body. Remember the purpose of training is to "stress" the various physiological systems of your body, force them to adapt and move you to a new level of fitness. When the athlete's body exceeds its capacity to cope with stress (from whatever source,) it is prone to infection or injury. Running with "dead" training shoes, i.e. the cushioning has been compressed and no longer absorbs the pounding of each stride, increases the likelihood of damage. A simple preventive measure is either to replace your shoes before they are totally destroyed or to use Sorbathane, a shoe insole that can reduces the forces absorbed by the body. Training too soon after a previous injury or illness also increases the likelihood of either repeated damage or a new problem emerging. A significant jump in the amount of running can overwhelm the body's ability to adapt. Training theory suggests that a 10% increase week over week allows this adaptation to occur without significant risk of injury.

What other factors can contribute to the injury?

Certainly the personality of the runner can have some bearing on the chance of sustaining an injury. A stubborn streak, one that refuses to yield to a fierce rainstorm or the pain from a gut-wrenching stitch, can be advantageous; it can help us break through barriers and explore the undiscovered territories of our athletic potential. Misdirected, however, it can force us to ignore the warning signs of a pending breakdown. Some athletes—perhaps those who are risk seekers, or maybe a touch obsessed with achieving a high mileage will choose to ignore the fatigue and high levels of soreness that often precede injury. The first tool for injury prevention is listening to what your body tells you!

The athlete's responses to injury

The athlete's belief systems and history with injuries can influence the way the damage is interpreted and the plan to recover from it. After the initial injury athletes tend to respond with a series familiar pattern:

The psychological phase is where the athlete is likely to experience a range of emotions that will vary according to the perceived severity of injury. Frustrations, tension, anger, disappointment, a loss of confidence and rampant uncertainty are common responses to injury. Depending on the athlete's experience, these responses will either be met with resignation or resilience. Injuries are never welcomed and attempting to put a positive spin on things in the initial stages of the injury only serves to deny the reality of this setback. There will be plenty of time to focus on a complete recovery, but the early stages that athlete should be allowed to work their way through whatever emotions they feel about this setback.

The analytical phase

Runners are an inquisitive breed of humanity. We are always studying how we feel and we often look for ways to improve our effort and performance. Inevitably, when an injury occurs we want to know why? How can we prevent it from happening again? What is the fastest path to recovery? What treatment do I need; the classic "rest-ice-compression—elevation," or a more advanced treatment using various therapies? What is my perceived rate of recovery? Will it take me days, weeks or months to recover?

The actual rate of recovery can be very different (often much quicker) than the perceived rate; thus it is important for the athlete to stay positive and motivated.

The behavioural response phase

Runners with a positive mind set toward the injury will quickly start a rehabilitation programme; the first part of which is the need to adjust their running goals. Some injuries present very uncertain timelines which make training and race plans uncertain. You can only plan around what you know; decide what you can and cannot do for training. If running is impossible can you swim, go cycling or do pool running? Perhaps those modes of exercise are not possible; what about weight training, or circuit training developing the uninjured areas. Getting back into activity as soon as is practically possible gives the athlete a sense of input (and maybe control) over their recovery; doing something is certainly more advantageous than doing nothing.

A feature of mentally tough athletes is not only their ability to persist despite discomforts and hardship, but also to attend rehabilitation with a consistent and committed approach. If you are injured as you read this article decide right now on your plan for recovery. Be mentally tough and work hard on the things that can help your recovery. Sitting back and letting nature do all the work is for the indolent, take an active role in your recovery and you may be surprised what happens.

The tactical "art of war"

Some athletes prefer to sit and kick. Others, are unabashed front runners wanting no company in their race. There are some athletes who will choose to execute a sustained surge to the finish line hoping to take the away the finishing speed of the sprinters. A few simply hope that they can hang onto the pace long enough to stay in the race. The perfect race can sometimes be an elusive cocktail of fitness and strategy. Correctly blended, and the performance can be truly memorable. Get one of those elements wrong and its bitter taste lingers. Never is the "recipe" the same for each race. As runners, we have to formulate our race plans, not only in anticipation of our rivals, but also in consideration of the weather, the course and distance. We all know athletes who had the fitness to win a particular race and yet made poor tactical decisions and underachieved.

Olympic history is replete with examples of athletes who won titles through the masterful application of their tactical plan—Sebastian Coe is a prime example. And then there are the stories of "favorites for the title" who can only look back and ask: "Why did I do that?" At the Los Angeles Olympics (1984) women marathon runners were advised that there would be furnace like conditions during the race. Most athletes, including heavily favored Grete Waitz (6 time winner of the New York marathon) who ran the early parts of the race cautiously. But as the thermometer failed to reach its feared height the more cautious athletes were forced to recognise that Joan Benoit had built up an unassailable lead. Benoit's correct tactical assessment of what was needed to win this race had secured her the Olympic title.

Keeping to a strict tactical plan requires faith in its design, patience in its execution and an unwavering commitment to see it through until the end. When an opponent races off far into the distance the seeds of self-doubt can easily undermine an athlete's plan. The successful athlete rises above this and stays confident that their plan will work. Paula Radcliffe's world record breaking performance of last year is an example of tactical excellence. Working to a meticulously detailed plan brought this athlete magnificent prize in her stellar career.

Historical examples aside, how as athletes can we improve our tactics during our races? An interesting reference book on tactics is Sun Tzu's "The Art of War". Written 2000 years ago by a Chinese warrior philosopher, this book offers a remarkable insight into the strategies and tactics of performance. Sun Tzu stated that *"victory in war is not repetitious, but adapts its form endlessly."* A runner's plan should never be predictable. When an athlete's performance becomes predictable they are better understood by their rivals who in turn adapt their strategies for success.

Prior to breaking the World 800m record Sebastian Coe had experimented with a variety of tactics. These included fast first laps (48-50 seconds), slow first laps (58 -60 seconds), mid race surges, accelerations over the last 100m of the race. The rehearsal of these tactics, which were generally in low key races, enabled Coe to either respond to, or dictate, the tactics of the race. When Coe raced he was never predictable.

In examination of another tactic Sun Tzu stated *"defence is for times of insufficiency. Attack is for times of surplus."* Tactics in sport convey a message and as an athlete you can either send the message or try to interpret it. If you are below your usual level of fitness you might chose a tactic that confuses your rivals and doesn't expose your weakness. Assertive tactics, front running for example, issues the "beat me if you can" ultimatum. Clearly this should only be used if you have the fitness and confidence to carry it off.

Any athlete who has competed in a distance race will identify with the thoughts, the doubts, perhaps even the fear that arises when someone throws in an unexpected surge. How long will it last? Should I go with them? Is it too soon or will I be making my move too late? The great Kenyan and Ethiopian runners of the 1990's have revolutionized running through both front running and devastating mid race surges. It is not uncommon for them to inject almost a 4 minute mile into the race mid way through a 10k. If surging is to be one of your chosen tactics, I believe that it would be most effective when delivered with an element of deception. Sun Tzu stated that *"a military operation involves deception. Even though you are competent appear to be incompetent, though effective appear to be ineffective."* Deceive your rivals by surging at a point in the race that makes them question whether you are really fit enough to maintain this pace, or is this just an act of desperation? Only you will know the answer.

Sun Tzu even offered some good old practical training and racing advice. *"When your forces are dulled, and your supplies are gone, then others will take advantage of your debility and rise up."* Knowing when to race and when to rest, that too is part of a sound tactical plan.

To be a successful athlete requires sound physical preparation, mental fortitude, and the tactical skill to deliver your performance. Of course the reality is that there are no magic formulas for success. But if Sun Tzu were around today he might also suggest that one of the most effective weapons against bad tactics is better tactics!

Stress: The Good, The Bad and The Ugly

The very mention of the word stress in our modern society evokes images of worry lines, tense faces and irritable dispositions; many would say that it is something that pervades almost every aspect of our daily experience. It has become a social phenomenon (at least, in the Western culture) that has spawned a multi-million pound business in the pharmaceutical and counseling industries

In the 1950's psychologist Hans Selye forwarded a theory that, to this day, shapes our thinking on the way that human body responds to stress. He suggested that stress was a series of *"psycho-physiological responses to any influence that disturbs a persons inner-balance."* Although the term stress is generally used to describe our behaviours and thoughts in response to situations, Selye also recognised that the physiology of stress is an essential response of our body to help us cope with challenges.

The physiological responses of the body to stress

For exercise physiologists, stress is a complex series of chemical and neurological reactions to a stimulus—the "stressor." With on-going exposure to these stressors, the athlete's body will adapt. All the training that we do, the various ways that we challenge our energy systems and muscles, all are designed to "stress" the body and force it to improve (i.e. get fitter). It is in this context that some physiologists have applied the term "Eustress"—or good stress.

Selye's "General Adaptation Theory" (GAS) stated that the body responds to stress in three distinct phases. The first response is known as the alarm phase which is where the body recognises that a demand has been placed upon it (e.g. a race is about to start, or, you are heading out on a training run.) Energy resources are mobilised and various chemicals (such as adrenaline) activate the physiological systems to meet the body's needs (the heart beats faster, breathing rate increases, etc). This has also been called the fight or flight response.

The second stage, the adaptation phase, is where the athlete's body adjusts to the repeated exposure to the stressor (e.g. in the race it might be the need to cope with fatigue, or in training, the way athlete prepares). If the athlete doesn't modify the stimulus—i.e. how hard they run, their fitness level will stay the same (plateau). Changing the intensity, the frequency of training, the duration of effort and the type of training (i.e. aerobic runs, or short anaerobic sprints, etc) will force the body to continue to adapt.

The final stage in Selye's theory is known as the exhaustion phase. If an athlete trains too hard they may experience difficulty adapting. The warning signs are initially subtle, then more direct. The athlete may experience low energy, persistent soreness, colds, etc. The mental fatigue is characterised by a waning interest in running. Certainly any one of these symptoms in isolation does not necessarily mean the athlete is at the exhaustion stage. Runners trying to adapt to a heavy training load will feel tired, however, when all of these symptoms are present the athlete is priming themselves for breakdown with an injury or illness.

The athletes's psychological response to stress

There is a line in John Milton's famous poem, *"Paradise Lost,"* that is an apt description of the various ways that runners interpret stress: *"the mind in itself can make a Hell of Heaven, and a Heaven of Hell."* The same race can be a source of extreme uncertainty for one runner and a yet provide a thrilling challenge for another. Key to the athlete's interpretation of the situation is their perception of competence. This perception is a blend of confidence, assessment of the competition and the degree of challenge. If you have done the training, raced competitively with confidence, have set your goals realistically, it is likely that you will feel that you "belong" in the race.

The psychological reactions to stress also follows Selye's three stages. Consider this scenario: *The athlete has had a poor preparation for a race. Weeks of injury have placed doubts in his mind, should he even race? The athlete is called to his marks.* Anxious thoughts (*"will I run well? Will my injury prevent me from doing my best?"*) will characterise the alarm response. The athlete's confidence may falter on the start line. Adrenaline is probably causing those metaphorical butterflies to dance in his stomach.

The gun is fired and the runners tear away at a blistering pace. Our athlete is already struggling. The runner tries to employ any psychological techniques to help him through the doubts that are inhibiting his performance. Coping with fading confidence, focusing on running technique, trying to block feelings of discomfort, channeling thoughts of mental toughness toward the race are skills used in the adaptation stage.

If the athlete fails to adapt to the psychological stress and reaches the exhaustion stage there are several likely outcomes: the runner drops out of the race, or, the athlete completes the race but suffers from the experience. The psychological damage that occurs when an athlete reaches the exhaustion stage can be difficult to heal. Rest and focusing on running enjoyment are the initial stages to help this athlete overcome setbacks and disappointment.

The Roman philosopher Epecitus once wrote " *men are not disturbed by things but by views they take of them.*" Good or bad (or ugly) stress is an undeniable part of lives but we can learn to use it to our advantage or allow it to inhibit our performance.

The Athens Olympic Games were fine showcase of many outstanding performances. The Olympic motto "Citius, Altius, Fortius"—swifter, higher, stronger—was embodied by athletes who proved to us that they are the pick of the human gene pool. Many were the epitomy of a supreme model for movement; a blend of speed and grace, athleticism and technique. But occasionally the Olympic Games will throw out a raw, almost jarring exception to the rule: an athlete short on style but high on talent; an athlete who seems to defy the conventional logic that technique is critical to performance. This is the story of runner with dreadful technique and an indomitable will. Deprivation and political excommunication could not suppress his desire to be the best in the world...

"The Locomotive" and the record books

In 1948 a diminutive Czech runner called Emil Zatopek bemused the running scene with his appalling style but brilliant performances. He quickly earned several nicknames: "The Locomotive," "The Bouncing Czech," and the less charitable moniker, "The Beast of Prague!" He was a runner taut with muscle and sinew but possessed the balletic poise of a prop forward attempting a pirouette. With his crunched shoulders and faced contorted in pain, Zatopek conveyed the look of a runner barely able to complete the next step. He was, however, fueled by an insatiable desire to prove to the world of athletics that determination is indeed a defining quality when it comes to racing. It could be argued that nobody had more determination than Emil Zatopek (number 3).

Zatopek's introduction to running could not have been more propitious. At the age of 19 he was employed in a state run shoe factory and a condition of employment was participation in a fitness run. Several hundred employees begrudgingly lined up for a 1500m race. Zatopek was reluctant to run but decided that if he had to run, he might as well run to win. Zatopek claimed 2nd place (and somewhere in the Czech Republic a retired factory worker will still claim that he once beat one of the greatest runners in the world!) Emil's talent for running was quickly identified and he was made to join the army; from there the state would control his career.

In 1948 the London Olympic Games were held; a brave attempt at normalcy after years of suffering. Zatopek—whose was fluent in 6 languages—was not only a great athlete but was clearly a man with a deep humanitarian commitment. He was quoted as saying *"after all those dark days of the war, the bombing, the killing, the starvation, the revival of the Olympic Games was as if the sun had come out. Suddenly, there were no more barriers, no more frontiers. Just the people meeting together."* Zatopek won the first of his many Olympic medals by claiming gold in the 10,000m and a silver in the 5,000m. Many athletes would consider that to be the highlight of their career, a feat they would never repeat. But "The Locomotive" was just getting started; with unbelievably hard training as his fuel, he was building up a head of steam and he carefully made his plans to rip the world of athletics asunder.

In 1952, Zatopek approached the zenith of his career. The Helsinki Olympic Games afforded him the opportunity to stake his place in athletic history and he knew that he would have to be supremely fit. His training—60 repetitions of 400m at 60 seconds—was at an intensity that few could imagine let alone cope with. Zatopek understood that physical preparation was only one component of his preparation, he would need to train his mind to cope with the extreme demands he would place on his body. *"When a person trains once, nothing happens. When a person forces himself to do a thing a hundred or a thousand times, then he has certainly developed in more ways than physical...Then willpower will be no problem."*

At the 10,000m race, Zatopek was quite simply unstoppable. Despite the attempts of his rivals to break the Czech's natural rhythm, Zatopek executed a race of remarkable pace judgement and won the title with ease. The

Locomotive was tearing around the track: Next stop, the 5000m.

In this race Zatopek faced England's Chris Chataway, a young runner in good form, the mercurial Gordon Pirie (who would soon be breaking world records), Alain Mimoun of France (who was to claim a gold medal in the marathon at the Melbourne Olympics 4 years later) and the German, Herbert Schade. This proved to be an absorbing contest. Each runner seemed determined to stamp their authority on the race and the lead changed constantly. Surges were met with counter-attacks, relaxed running was followed by intense changes of pace; each athlete trying to position themselves for the final sprint for the line. Schade led at the bell but Zatopek—the agony written across face mistakenly suggesting that he was a spent force—struck for home. Zatopek's trademark grimace must have given encouragement to his rivals for they sensed a weakening of their prey and prepared to pounce. With 300m to run, Chataway unleashed his sprint but was followed stride for stride by Schade. Zatopek fell in behind and was himself passed by Mimoun who charged to the front. The Helsinki crowd stood to their feet; this was high drama, electrifying the senses. Who would win?

Around the final bend Mimoun held the lead but with Schade still poised to challenge. Chataway took the inside lane and tragically clipped the track inner rail; he came crashing down onto the track. The crowd roared ever louder. Seemingly out of nowhere, Zatopek sprinted past everybody. With his arms thrashing wildly he drew on that battery of willpower and propelled himself to victory.

A few days later, Zatopek sealed Olympic immortality when he claimed his 3rd Gold medal (at one games) by winning the marathon title. Zatopek's wife, Danova, also celebrated Olympic victory when she claimed the javelin title.

After he retired from serious competitive running, Zatopek faced some troubling and uncertain times. He was an outspoken critic of the Soviet suppression of a Czech up-rising (1968). Consequently, he was sent to a uranium mine for 6 years and was forced to complete menial tasks. His spirit, however, was unbroken and in an act of selfless generosity, he donated one of his gold medals to the Australian Ron Clarke who had broken many world records but had not won an Olympic title. In 1975, Zatopek was honoured by the United Nations with the

International Fair-Play Prize.

Beauty and grace were highly valued features of movement at the ancient Olympic Games, but it is not hard to imagine the Gods of Olympus enjoying the irony that one of their greatest athletes, ever, would be the antithesis of this ideal.

Natural rhythms and sports performance

Have you ever gone for an afternoon run and found that no matter how hard you try, you are having a lousy run. You know you are fit, you feel rested and yet something does not seem to be right. Your stride is awkward, you feel heavy and lacking in energy. The next day you decide to start your training before lunch and you have a fabulous run. You feel fluent and find it hard to believe that there could be such a difference. What could possible explain such performance variation?

Chronobiology, the science of biological rhythms, offers some fascinating insights into how our body functions change throughout the day (or even longer periods). This field is not to be confused with Biorhythms which are like a physiological version of astrology, i.e. there is no scientific proof that they exist.

Natural biological rhythms are important functions in our existence. Although humans can exercise some influence over some of these rhythms, they are internally (also called endogenously) generated. There are rhythms in our body that are repeated in a 24 hour cycle—Ultradian rhythms—and they include: heart beats, breathing, body temperature, hormone production and blood pressure variance to name a few. The most obvious rhythm is the sleep-wake cycle and this is sometimes called a circadian rhythm. The word circadian is taken from the Latin "circa diem" meaning about a day.

There are also natural rhythms that take longer than 24 hours—Infradian rhythms—this includes the menstrual cycle which repeats in a 28 day cycle. For men, it has been suggested, that beard growth rates change over a 45 day cycle. There is also some evidence that suggests weight loss and gain may correspond to seasonal (and thus temperature) fluctuations.

How do these rhythms effect running performance?

Body temperature is known to rise and fall throughout the 24 hour cycle—sometimes by as much as 1.5 degrees. This represents a significant shift in the basal metabolic rate—the rate at which the athlete's body consumes energy- and there seems to be a strong connection to body temperature and performance. Racing or training at peak body temperatures—late afternoon, or early evening, seems to suit athletic tasks that require a high degree of skill, e.g. sprinting races. Marathon racing not only requires the athlete to efficiently produce and manage energy production, but it also requires the athlete to tolerate and disperse (through sweating) the heat that is generated. As lower body temperatures are experienced in the morning, training and racing at this time may be preferable for an athlete that struggles with thermoregulation.

All athletes recognise the need for a warm-up. Raising the body temperature helps to increase muscle viscosity; it gives the muscles increased flexibility and range of movement in the joints. Coinciding with the rhythmic lows of body temperature, athletes seem to have an increased exposure to injury as muscle tone—which also seems to follow a rhythmic pattern—is poor early in the morning. Thus, if you have to race early in the morning, you will have to train your body to adapt to the demands of running at such a time.

The adrenal cortex—a small structure sitting on top of our kidneys—is responsible for releasing a number of chemicals that can influence athletic performance. The role of adrenaline is well documented in the lay-press, less recognised is the role of the steroidal hormone Cortisol. Also known as the stress hormone, Cortisol is released by the body in response to physical or psychological stress and it can help the athlete to cope with the challenges of exercise. Cortisol plays an important role in cardiovascular function and carbohydrate metabolism and is released in a circadian rhythm with peaks early in the morning and lows in the evening.

The athlete's liver is known to regulate glycogen—the stored form of sugar—in a circadian rhythm. When the body utilizes its stores of glucose in the blood, it asks the liver to convert glycogen into glucose. These stores of glycogen peak in the late morning but dip—significantly—in the late afternoon.

Another rhythm that naturally occurs is the Postprandial dip. This is where measures such as muscles strength and general energy seem to drop the early afternoon before picking up in the later. Other physiological measures e.g. flexibility, power output, also seemed to peak later in the day.

So what is the best time to train and race?

Some of this information seems contradictory. Do you run late at night to take advantage of the body temperature variance? But isn't the runner's cortisol rhythm at a low thus impeding the adaptation for training effects or assistance in metabolizing carbohydrates? So perhaps you should race in the morning, but didn't I just say that muscle tone is poor and the risk of injury is high? Undoubtedly the effects of these rhythms are blended, some have greater dominance than others but each of these are subject to individual variance.

Some runners are brilliant at times when other athletes always struggle; but what if you have to race at a time when you know that you are often low? Are these rhythms a blessing or curse?

Ask yourself this question: Do you always struggle at a certain time? Why not keep a diary and look for evidence of your patterns. Even though we might struggle to overcome the effect of some of these rhythms, the runner's body has the amazing capacity to adapt to changes imposed upon it. Practising at times of a low may give the athlete the sense that they are masters of their own performance and not subject to the deleterious effects of the peaks and troughs associated with these rhythmic patterns.

Shakespeare in Love...With Running!

When William Shakespeare was a young man, like everyone, he was faced with difficult career choices. Not many people know that prior to his success with penmanship, he had tried his hand at Sports Psychology. However, his lyrical musings on sport did not attract mass appeal in Tudor England. Thus it came to pass that Sports Psychology's loss was English Literatures gain. Today, however, if you comb the voluminous works of The Bard, there are still many hints of Bill Shakespeare: Sports Psychologist.

"Nay, if you get it you shall get it with running" (King Lear). From the pinnacles of human achievement, to the depths athletic defeat, Shakespeare seemed to understand that complex emotions often accompany a running race. He understood running's power to shape character, to define the courage or failings of an athlete. As a sports psychologist, Shakespeare also knew that the mind could sabotage the possibility of a great performance: *"Our doubts are traitors, and make us lose the good we oft might win by fearing to attempt."*

Although there are many skills that an athlete needs to bring to the start line, a key skill is the determination to *"Fight till the last gasp."* Bill Shakespeare also believed that athletes who focused on their effort rather than outcome gained a strong sense of personal control over their performance: *"Things won are done. Joys soul lies in the doing."*

The nature versus nurture debate has perplexed scientists and philosophers for centuries: Are we born the way we are or does our environment (our experiences) create us? There is an old adage in coaching that bluntly states "you can't put in what God left out." Can a runner without talent train hard and become a successful runner? Shakespeare eloquently summarised his thoughts on this matter by stating: *"some are born great, some achieve greatness, and some have greatness thrust upon them."* He believed that *"we are such stuff as dreams are made on"* that is, athletes with immense self-belief and hard training can overcome a deficit in natural talent.

"Now bid me run and I will strive with things impossible" (Julius Caesar). Some athletes run with the purpose of participating; they run the race and take whatever

result it brings. But there are a few athletes who have a much more lofty goal: they strive to re define our perceptions of the attainable. In the late 1970's a Kenyan athlete named Henry Rono traveled to Europe with the record books firmly in his sights. He was the thin end of the wedge; a trickle of African athletes that would soon become a tidal wave of talent sweeping aside the best distance runners in the world. Rono was considered a man ahead of his time. With remarkable front running, he broke 4 four World records in a matter of weeks. His performances were so fast that many people believed that no-one would be able to improve on his times. Rono had taken the 5000m standard down to 13.06. Enter Haile Gebreselassie who has made Rono's feats seem quite ordinary by comparison. Shattering every conventional thought about pacing and endurance, Gebreselassie has taken the 5km record to a stratospheric 12.39. Will it end there? Unlikely; there will always be other athletes striving to achieve the impossible!

"No pain, no gain!" "When the going gets tough the tough get going!" Each of these cliches has become the rallying cry for athletes and armchair analysts. The reality of the struggle for our successes in sport and life is somehow tempered by the view that we can win if only we can cope with the pain. Shakespeare had already written about this; *"pain pays the income of each precious thing."* Certainly as runners we expect to have to fight our fatigue, face our fears, in order to meet the challenges of each race. In fact sometimes we feel robbed of the experience if the success comes too easily. The thrill of success often comes from staring down those personal demons and elevating our performance to previously considered unattainable levels. As Shakespeare alluded, it is the struggle, the pain that helps us to define ourselves and give meaning to our efforts.

If Shakespeare had stayed in Sports Psychology he might have written something like *"Let not your race be a Comedy of Errors."* He might have been honoured for his contributions to sport by having a race named after him: *"A MidSummers Night Dream Mile!"* But alas (*"poor Yoric"*) he didn't and lost to the world of sports science was a man with a keen understanding of the runner's soul.

Talking your way to success

When he stepped into the ring, everyone knew that Muhammed Ali, arguably the greatest boxer, ever, had arrived. Taunting his opponents, verbally sparring with the crowd, teasing the television cameras with promises of a quick knockout, Ali exuded a huge sense of presence in this sporting arena. He was an ebullient mix of cockerel and tiger, strutting and snarling on the stage. What was often interpreted as sporting hubris was also the action of a supremely confident athlete declaring to the world his heightened state of preparation and competition readiness. Muhammed Ali believed he was the master of his opponents, the master of the ring; although his verbal sophistry sometimes bordered on the eloquent it was clearly designed to intimidate. He used his words to unsettle his rivals, *"I'm so bad I make medicine sick!"* and put them on edge *"I'm going to float like a butterfly, sting like a bee."*

Ali recognized that bold statements, whether they are brash and extroverted, or almost subliminal, have powerful ways of enhancing performance. Sports psychology has labeled this phenomenon self-talk (also known as affirmation statements), it is described as *"an internal dialogue in which the individuals interpret feelings and perceptions,…and then give themselves instructions and reinforcement."*

Self-talk research studies have shown that athletes using such statements stay focused on the challenge and do not give a thought to past mistakes. They have been used to help an athlete's technical proficiency. The runner evaluates their form in the race, if feeling tense, or they are over-striding, etc, they might employ statements that concentrate on relaxation. The key is to give oneself specific instructions, *"okay, for the next mile of this marathon I am going to concentrate on bringing my breathing under control. I am going to have relaxed, easy flowing strides. I will not struggle, etc."* These strategies can also be used to help the athlete feel confident with their tactical choices. Doubts can quickly have a corrosive effect on the athlete's confidence, *"should I make my move now or wait a bit longer?"* Self-talk can help remind the runner of the tactical plan they have developed, it can reinforce the athlete's perception that things are going well.

While the crowds that support runners are often a welcome boost, sometimes the accompanying surge in adrenaline pushes the athlete into a pace that they are not able to sustain. Mental discipline to avoid this urge can be achieved through self-talk statements. Calming statements, focusing on effort control, pace distribution and relaxation can help a runner through such situations.

Self-talk statements can also help in the emotional control of the performance. Things don't always go to plan. When the runner that you have wanted to beat pulls away from you—yet again—it can send a range of emotions charging through your mind. Should I give up? What's the point?

I am curious to know of the thoughts of the Brazilian athlete—Vanderlei de Lima as he was leading the Athens Olympic Games marathon race. You will recall that in the latter stages of the race—with a 40 second lead—he was basically mugged by a spectator and pushed off the road and into the crowd. Credit to this athlete that he picked himself up and tried to re-gain his concentration. I can only speculate that he used self-talk statements to help him through this situation, however, his 3rd place finish was testament to impressive resilience and inner strength. Emotional control, whether it is to control anger or contain the excitement is needed if athletes are to realize their race potential.

What are the benefits of self-talk?

Two sports psychologists, Mallett and Hanrahn (1997) reported that self-talk statements significantly improved the performance of sprinters. They found that these athletes were better able to execute their skill and exert more emotional control when they talked themselves through their race before it started. Exactly how does self-talk work? Back to Muhammed Ali—a man whose use of sports psychology was decades ahead of his peers. "It's *the repetition of affirmations that leads to belief. And once that belief becomes a deep conviction, things begin to happen.*" When the self-talk has a motivational component it enhances confidence, helps the athlete to monitor their effort input (i.e. preventing the "too fast, too soon" syndrome that plagues neophyte marathon runners) and helps to create positive moods. But does this really help? Well research is increasingly showing that it does, what is equally evident is that no amount of negative thinking has ever been proven to improve performance. As Muhammed Ali would put it "*I figured that if I said it enough, I would convince the world that I really was great.*"

Success: It's all in your imagination!

It's a Sunday morning long run and you find yourself locked into an easy rhythm. The miles are flowing by and your thoughts start to drift. You imagine what it would be like to be the best runner in the world. You sweep aside all challengers with imperious ease, no, that's too easy; you decide to heroically clinch victory with the last stride of the race. You blow kisses to the crowd, no, that's not your style, either. You modestly accept their applause and politely field the questions from the admiring masses. A you a legend in your own mind?

A bracing wind sweeping down from the north (where else does it come from!) and the sight of a champion athlete effortlessly striding across your path snaps you out of your medal-filled reverie. "*What's the point of dreaming,*" you say to yourself, "*I'll never be that good!*" You wipe your runny nose with your shirt sleeve, tilt your head into the wind and try to concentrate on finishing this run with a bit of self-respect.

Why not imagine what it would be like to be the best? Carl Sagan, the science fiction writer once wrote "*Imagination will often carry us to worlds that may never exist, but without it we go nowhere.*" If imagination is the destination, then mental imagery techniques are the methods of travel. It has been well-documented that our thoughts, then images, create neuromuscular impulses that bring about a response. Writers and philosophers have long exploited this connection; they know only too well that imagination creates physical responses in the body—it's what DH Lawrence in "*Lady Chatterley's Lover*" relied on to help sell books! It is what Dale Carnegie used to help people acquire positive work habits; "*whether you think you can, or think you can't, you're right!*" The implications for runners are clear: Since our bodies tend to do what they are told, all we need to decide is what to tell them.

How to use mental imagery

There are two distinct forms of mental imagery; internal and external, and they can be used to develop many psychological skills. Internal imagery has been described as where the athlete "*actually imagines and feels the sensations that might be expected when competing in a situation,*" (Mahoney). External imagery is where the person " *views themselves from the perspective of an external observer,*" i.e. you see yourself running.

Mental imagery has been beneficial in helping athletes trying to learn a complex skill. It is not uncommon to see athletes competing at the highest level close their eyes before the start of their event. If you closely look at their body movements, you can almost see them executing their run, jump or throw even though they haven't taken a step. They are imagining themselves conquering the challenge before them and their muscles seem to twitch accordingly.

If the athlete has identified a flaw in their running technique, they may use mental imagery to make the necessary correction. Using both internal and external techniques, the athletes might picture themselves running the race with power, style, and relaxed effort (external imagery). It is as if you are watching a movie of yourself and what you see is what you want and wish for. The internal imagery will concentrate on picturing yourself actually doing the event, not watching it. You imagine yourself feeling confident and able to respond to the challenges of your rivals.

For several years I used external imagery techniques in my training. I always wanted to win the race easily and I thought that if I practised hard enough, and imagined winning with a clear picture, that would do it. But it seemed that every race that I imagined was a battle to the line with an equally determined rival. After awhile I started to imagine races where I would see myself giving every ounce of effort and holding my form (technique) until the end. These were things that I could control and I felt that they gave me an edge in my performances.

Mastering emotions using mental imagery

Emotions can have a powerful effect on a runner's performance. A lack of emotion may produce a flat performance, while excessive emotion may contribute to a lack of control over the skills that are needed to compete well. Mental imagery can be used to give the athlete the sense that they are controlling all aspects of their behaviour and performance. They may imagine themselves as calm, quietly confident, with complete focus on their task. Or, they might prefer—according to their style—to see themselves as brash, bold and intense. Whatever your imagined outcome, repeated use of mental imagery will help you to acquire these skills.

One of the advantages of using mental imagery training is that it can challenge your attitudes and perceptions of your abilities. If you are trying to break personal barriers, imagery can move you from pre-conceived ideas to new systems of self-belief. Outcome expectancy—believing that you are capable of great things—is reinforced when you use these techniques.

Tips for practicing mental imagery

- Practise in a quiet place for 5—10 minutes.
- Try external imagery first. See yourself running with your current technique and level of fitness. Imagine things that you can control: your effort, the energy that you can bring to the run, an efficient technique.
- Repeat this process every day for a week. Consider a regular part of your overall training.
- Once you are in a mental training routine, identify some areas that you would like to improve. May be it is an improvement in your choice of race tactics, perhaps it is some aspect of emotional control.
- Incorporate the desired change into your imagery and practise, regularly.
- After 2 weeks of using external imagery, try to develop internal imagery techniques. In a 10 minute session do 5 minutes of each technique. Increasing the amount of time spent practicing these skills can only help to reinforce the positive benefits.

Will mental imagery work? As Muhammed Ali once said *"The man that has no imagination has no wings."*

The Summit of Athletic Achievement

The great poet Robert Browning once wrote *"ah, but a man's reach exceed his grasp or what's a heaven for."* In 1956 a short, bespectacled runner named Christopher Brasher extended his athletic reach toward the Melbourne Olympic Games. His chance for success in his chosen event—the 3000m steeplechase—was rated slim to none. He had never won a national championship, his contributions to running at the international level had been enthusiastic but certainly not stellar; and although immensely strong, Brasher possessed average speed. He barely qualified for the British team (behind John Disley and Eric Shirley).

Chris Brasher, however, was a man who always seemed destined to make an impact, to leave a footprint on society. He was called a man with a bucaneering persona, a raconteur, a ceaseless advocate for issues that he believed in; but he was a man with—by all accounts—an ordinary talent in running. How can this be? This man won an Olympic Gold medal. Chris Chataway—the great 5000m runner—once whimsically summarised Brasher's talents: *"He is 5% ability, 95% guts!"*

To understand more of Chris Brasher's achievements and the personality of this man we have to leave the running track and head for the rugged slopes of the world's great mountain ranges. Mountaineering and running have much in common. Taking risks are an inseparable feature of both sports; these risks, some might call opportunities, carry great intrinsic rewards; the satisfaction of conquering the most difficult of challenges. They require you to face your fear and brook no compromise. They can be solitary sports that test the mettle of the athlete. It was on the granite slopes and ledges of many tough mountains, and on the cinder tracks of England, that Brasher forged the temperament that would drive him to success throughout his life.

Brasher had a great talent for climbing and was selected as the first reserve for a team that eventually conquered Mt. Everest. Brasher may have missed out on participating in one of the great accomplishments in history but within a year he was given another chance. Acting as pacemaker, Chris Brasher helped to propel Roger Bannister to run under four minutes for 1 mile. Bannister's achievement was incomparable and it is not surprising that Brasher started to feel that his desire for personal achievement would forever live in the shadows of the famous day in May, 1954. "*I wanted, and needed, to prove something to myself,*" said Brasher; and so he turned his attention to the Melbourne Olympic Games— 1956.

Brasher received the expert tutelage of Franz Stampfl, the legendary coach who had guided Roger Bannister towards his great races. Stampfl placed Brasher on a programme rich with interval training and a heavy emphasis on aerobic conditioning. The plan was meticulously designed to have Brasher reach his peak at the 3000m steeplechase final. While his teammates, Disley and Shirley were struggling with illness and injury, Brasher was quietly rounding into the form of his life.

There were two formidable opponents in the steeplechase final: Ernst Larsen from Norway and the Hungarian, Sandor Rozsnyol. Larsen immediately stated his intentions for the race by surging into the lead. He had established a gap of 15m by the first kilometre and he looked in impressive form. The world record holder, Rozsnyol, tracked the leader and also appeared to be comfortable with the pace. Brasher seemed like an anonymous participant; one of those spectral characters that leave little impact on the race other than the appearance of their name on the entry sheet. However, as each lap unfolded Brasher steadily moved through the field until at the bell lap, he was positioned to take the lead.

All of the tactical manoeuvring of the favourites had played right into the hands of Brasher. Larsen was struggling to cope with the effects of his impetuous front running, Rozsnyol also seemed to lack the zip that had defined his world record breaking runs. Brasher surged into the lead and with each step pulled on the strength that he had garnered on the slopes of the Himalayas and the Alps. He started to move away from his rivals. The gold medal was his. Brasher ran 8.41.2 beating his best by 6 secs—he had reached his peak performance in the race that mattered the most.

Hours later the victory was taken away as Brasher was disqualified for "interfering with another athlete."

In move that is hard to imagine in today's Olympics, Larsen and Rozsnyol lobbied the judges to have Brasher re-instated. They said that he had not impeded them and it was not fair that Brasher not be awarded the gold medal. The appeal took many hours to process, eventually the judges reversed their decision and awarded the victory to Brasher. When news that he had won the race reached England, his clubmates sent him a telegram, *"Well done the old scrubber!"*

Meanwhile, Brasher had been initially drowning his sorrows then celebrating his re-instatement; thus, he became one of the few Olympic athletes to receive a medal in a completely inebriated state: *"I was completely blotto and had an asinine grin on my face."* Brasher retired after this race even though Franz Stampfl believed that his athlete could run under 8.30 for that event.

Many people would happily fade into obscurity after a modicum of the success that Brasher had enjoyed; but he was yet to make an even greater contribution. In 1979 he participated in the New York marathon. Brasher was energised by the experience and saw an opportunity to bring running to the masses. In 1981 he—along with John Disley—overcame immense bureaucratic obstacles to launch the London Marathon. It was an overwhelming success and over the years has produced not only some of the finest marathon races of all time, but has helped to contribute millions of pounds to charity.

Chris Brasher, sadly, passed away in February, 2003. As a man who appreciated literature, Brasher would have loved the poignancy of Browning's quote. Throughout his life, Brasher had aimed high and celebrated its spirit to the full. He was an inspiring example for all.

Psyching yourself up for a great race

A sage once said *"the eyes are the windows of the soul."* If that person had been a running coach, he might have added *"the eyes are also the study of the athlete's state of mental preparation."* Compare the gazes of two of Britain's greatest athletes: Linford Christie—eyes firmly fixed on the finishing line, narrow focus, burning with intensity. Nothing will distract him, his eyes barely blink thus avoiding the risk of breaking his concentration. Then there is the relaxed focus of Paula Radcliffe. Her eyes calm, looking at the course and setting her sights on the challenges that will slowly unfold over 26 miles. Those who interpret that calm as weakness do so at their peril! The stares match the body language and both send a message that the athlete is ready to compete.

It doesn't take an astute observer, however, to pick up on the insecurity and anxiety teasing the minds of runners that display a general lack of confidence. These are runners who perform with tense muscles as if they were a puppet controlled by steel strings. There is almost a cruel inevitability that they will not perform to expectations.

What mental skills help athlete's like Linford Christie or Paula Radcliffe achieve such high levels of performance? Firstly, there is an inherent degree of self-confidence. Built on this foundation are a complex set of skills that may include highly developed visualisation training and mental relaxation techniques. But just like an athlete who has trained hard and then attempts to race without an adequate warm-up, these mental skills cannot be effectively applied without the athlete *"psyching themselves up."*

This phrase has worked its way into the language of many sports and is the mental equivalent of a warm up. It can take different forms for athletes from different sports. For weightlifters a firm slap around the face, a snort of sniffing salts and lots of shouting helps to prepare them for an intense burst of energy. The need to supercharge the system with adrenaline may be appropriate for a weightlifter or track sprinter but for a distance runner it could lead to irrational decision making and poor pace judgement. Given the measured release of a distance runner's effort, their style of *"psyching up"* may take a quiet, more reflective approach.

Sports psychology has investigated this phenomenon and uses the term "arousal" to describe varying states of physical and mental preparation. The relationship between arousal and performance forms what is known as the "inverted "U" hypothesis." According to this idea an athlete with low arousal is likely to achieve a low level of performance. For example, an athlete that shows up at the race a few minutes before start, doesn't warm-up, and hasn't spared a thought for the race details—how they will face the tough parts of the race, etc,—will not achieve their race potential.

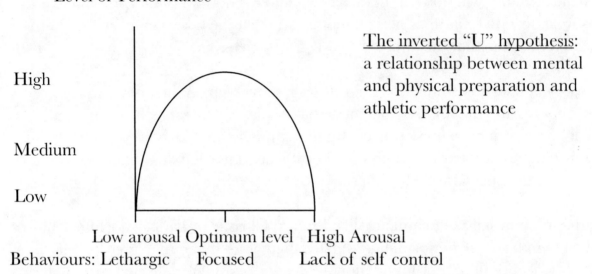

At the peak of the inverted U is the optimum level of arousal and performance. This is where the athlete has mentally focused their energy with control toward the demands of the event. They have physically warmed up, and have mentally planned for the challenges of the race. They have anticipated at what part of the race things may become difficult and they know how they will respond. They have considered the tactics of their rivals and have decided where they will make their "move". These athletes calmly await the start of the race.

What is particularly interesting about the "inverted U" is the idea that performance will actually decrease with excessive arousal—i.e. you can "*psych yourself up*" too much. These athletes fail to control their thoughts and become tense with anticipation.

What techniques can you use to help you "psych yourself up"? Self-talk can be a useful approach to achieve this optimum arousal state. This is where the athletes remind themselves of all the positive things about their training, their racing and their personal qualities that will help them to perform well when the race starts. This is a technique that attempts to focus the athlete's thoughts on either creating or drawing out confidence before the start.

Visualisation is another technique that can be used to help bring the athlete to a heightened state of readiness. This is where the athlete creates a picture in their mind of themselves running. It is important that the athlete practises "seeing" things that are within their control—i.e. their running form and technique.

Some athletes resort to other, more practical, techniques to complete their race preparation. Listening to music "Walkmans" may be used to distract an anxious athlete from their thoughts or it may be used to energise them. Some runners have used cold showers before the race hoping the sensory stimulation will activate body and mind for performance.

Whichever technique you decide to use, incorporate it into your training and practise it just as you would with your physical training: regularly and with commitment. When you race you can draw on these skills and it will seem like a natural part of your race preparation. Let the results take care of themselves!

Attempted murder at The White City

In 1954 a Soviet runner (Ukrainian) burst onto the scene with a terrifying instinct for destruction. Perhaps it was the years of deprivation while serving as a prisoner of war, or maybe it was the incessant indoctrination he received while serving in the Russian Navy, either way, Vladimir Kuts brought a ruthless quality to track racing. In an era of polite handshakes and courteous exchanges, Kuts must have felt like an angry wind of revolution blowing into the face of the athletic establishment.

Embracing Russian President Nikita Kruschev's demand that *"all World records must be taken by Soviet athletes,"* Kuts was identified as a talented athlete and was pushed into a heavy training programme. Running 20 miles a day, sometimes in combat boots and sometimes carrying a sandbag over his shoulders, Kuts honed his fitness to a level that promised great performances. He duly delivered. In August, 1954, Kuts claimed the 5000m World record (13:56.6) in winning the European Championship.

It was apparent that Kuts was a maverick runner the like the sport had never seen before. His tactics bore no compromise and were suggestive of a hunter culling his prey. He would start a 10km race with a 60 second first lap; a strategy that even today's athletes would find extravagant. He would run slow, then fast, then even faster laps; all the while his strides seemingly mocking his rivals. All who attempted to challenge his superiority invited ruthless counter-attacks. He was a ceaseless, determined athlete with World conquest on his mind.

Vladimir Kuts—A ruthless frontrunner!

The silver medallist at that European championship was Christopher Chataway—a young Oxford student enjoying one of the finest seasons in his stellar career. Chataway was an ebullient character with a taste for the odd cigar and scholarly pursuits. He was the perfect foil to Vladimir Kuts. While Kuts was being pushed to intolerable levels of fatigue in training and racing (too often he was taken away from the track on a stretcher), Chataway was finding ways to squeeze the maximum amount of benefit from the minimum amount of effort.

Chataway's season had started in May, 1954 with the pacemaking duties for Roger Bannister's seminal performance over the mile. Chataway went onto to claim the Empire Games 3 mile title in Vancouver, and then followed this with a silver medal at the European Championship (defeating the amazing Emil Zatopek). As the season drew to a close an unlikely invitational match—London versus Moscow—brought these two great athletes together for a race of historic proportions. Chataway versus Kuts: a clash of form and fluency versus drive and aggression.

The White City Stadium in North West London no longer exists, but in 1954 it was the heartbeat of British Athletics. On a damp October evening 60,000 spectators poured into the stands; they were not sure what to expect: would the 5000m race feature an attempted "murder" by the Russian sailor or could Chataway find some way to cling to the pace?

Kuts lined up on the start line looking as intense as ever. He was dressed in a blood red Russian singlet with the hammer and sickle emblem on his chest bluntly reminding us that sport and ideology were the new weapons in The Cold War that had just started. Kuts was the epitomy of Nikita Krushchev's "*man of the future today*."

Chataway had developed great speed throughout the season. He had pushed the great John Landy to a new World record in the mile—the only question that remained was whether he had the strength to endure Kuts' inevitable surges and withering pace.

The first mile was reached in 4mins 24 and Kuts, predictably, was forcing the pace. Chataway had one, very simple strategy: stick to Kuts like a limpet and then out sprint him over the final few metres. Kuts was a runner whom did not like company and he repeatedly tried to shake off his rival with his trademark surges.

The second mile was completed in 8mins 54 and still Chataway stuck to the heels of the Russian. Kuts unleashed a devastating sprint and then slowed. The Englishman followed. The pain contorting the faces of both runners suggested that the pace was exacting an awful toll on their bodies, but neither would yield.

Into the final two laps and Kuts once again tried to break the spirit of his rival. Years later, Chataway commented on that final half mile: "at that point.. *I had really given up hope. I was just living second by second…The final lap was terrible, terrible! Until that moment of hope in the last 50 metres.*"

There are times in a runner's life when they must look into their running soul and ask "*what kind of runner am I? One who gives up, or one that truly digs deep and squeezes every last ounce of effort in a race.*" The last 50 metres was such a watershed in Chataway's career. Kuts had failed to shake off his rival and now a furious sprint would answer all the questions. The crowd roared Chataway on. Kuts responded, Chataway pulled level, Kuts fought back. They were two great gladiators battling to the bitter end. Did Kuts falter or did Chataway pull on some hidden reserve? With the very last stride of the race Chataway nudged ahead and defeated the Russian; the time: a new World record, 13:51.6.

Ten days later, Kuts responded in the only way that he knew how: a new World record, 13:51.2.

This story has an unhappy ending. After winning the Rome Olympic 5000m title (yet another World record 13:35) Kuts was carried away on a stretcher. A very serious heart condition was identified and soon he would suffer a series of heart attacks. Aged 29, Kuts was told that he would never run again. He died—100lbs overweight—at the age of 48—a tragic end for a brilliant athlete.

Chataway went on to enjoy great success as a businessman and served as a cabinet minister in the government of Sir Edward Heath.

Faster times over the 5000m have been run, but it will be hard to imagine that a more absorbing contest between such interesting characters will ever grace our sport.

Mental toughness on the road to Hell!

After many months of training, tens of thousands of athletes recently took their fitness to the streets of London and faced that most difficult of running challenges: the marathon. As was expected, the crowd were treated to an intriguing and exciting spectacle; high performance running blended with participation, mid-race drama mixed with the circus theatrics of "juggling" runners. This was sport at its egalitarian best: the world's fastest runners placing their feet on the same start line as the Pantomime horse!

Despite the incredible support of the spectators, the desire to quit the race, ease off the pace or succumb to a "bad patch" effected some of the athletes that raced this distance. What separated those runners who enjoyed great personal success from those runners who were disappointed? Are those successful athletes simply immune to these doubts?

Mental toughness is an interesting concept in sports psychology. It is a quality that allows an athlete like Evans Ruttu of Kenya—the winner of this year's London race—to brush off a bad fall, mend a broken rhythm and position himself back in the pack of leading runners. It would have been easy for him to fixate on the scrapes and bruises but instead, he drew on his mental toughness to continue the race.

And then there is the story of Tracey Morris from Wales, winner of the women's London marathon race. She exercised amazing self-belief to emerge out of anonymity and claim an Olympic Games team spot. Dissenting voices might have given her no chance of success, but again, mental toughness allowed her physical training to be fully realised. These are just two exemplars of mental strength but, of course, they are not unique. These athletes, and others like them, recognise that effective racing requires you to train the body and sharpen the mind for the challenge.

How do you develop mental toughness?
Mental toughness is an interesting amalgam of many skills, some inherent in each athlete's personality. These skills include: determination, resilience, courage, confidence, and perseverance. Experience is undoubtedly a great

educator and these qualities, or lack of them, can be candidly exposed in a running race. Many of these skills have their origins in our running habits. Failing to finish running sessions, slowing down when the pace gets difficult, self defeating thoughts are all symptoms that may indicate the runner needs to adopt a new attitude if they wish to take their running to the next level. Bad training habits readily transfer into bad racing habits. Somehow you have to find a way to break this cycle.

The phrase "if you continue to do what you have always done, you will continue to get what you have always gotten," is particularly poignant for the reflective athlete. This suggests the need to try something different if you wish to break old habits or acquire new skills. Here are some very practical techniques that can be employed that can help a runner become a mentally tough athlete:

Set yourself a difficult challenge in training—but one that is realistic and attainable, then approach with the resolve to see it through. Refuse to yield! This challenge might not necessarily be performance related. You might decide to do a 6 a.m. run every morning for the next week. You may decide to abstain from something that you cherish (tea / beer / cakes, etc) for a set period; a runners version of Lent! Whatever it is that you choose, the purpose is to strengthen your will power and resolve.

Mental toughness is reinforced when you praise yourself for achieving your goals. Some running workouts might simply be focused on the mental skill rather than the benefits of hard effort. Example: I used to set myself a hill work of 6 x 60m hard sprints. After the 6 runs were completed, I would dedicate 1 extra run for mental toughness—even though I had given my all on the previous 6 runs. I imagined my rivals doing the same workout and I knew that they would finish at 6 repetitions. I wanted them to "know" that I was prepared to push myself that much harder and that I had the "edge" over them. Such strategies were repeated over and over until that mental toughness became an automatic skill. When it came to race situations the confidence and resilience seemed to come naturally.

Practise being mentally tough before the race. Sometimes an athlete has to face a few personal demons—the little whispers in the mind that want you to believe that you haven't trained hard enough. These are insidious thoughts that drain an athlete's confidence. Affirmation statements—"I have trained hard and I am ready," could be repeated over and over in your mind. Those negative thoughts are the enemy, refuse to give them any voice.

Design your race plan. Include, not only tactics, but anticipate where the greatest mental challenges will come from. Experienced runners in the Boston marathon know that the infamous Heartbreak Hill is where many athletes have struggled. With sound preparation and anticipation, an athlete can concentrate on the skills that will help them overcome the challenge rather than folding under the pressure.

Whether you be Olympic athlete or Pantomime horse mental toughness is an integral part of our sport. Learn and apply these skills. Be tough! You deserve the rewards of all your hard training!

A Breath of Fresh Air

The Olympic weightlifter stands before the bar and closes his eyes. He concentrates, relaxes his arms before gripping the bar. With a powerful outburst of energy he hoists the bar onto his chest. Three quick short breaths then one deep breath. As he pushes the bar upward he exhales. It is a successful lift. The Olympic distance runner settles into the early laps of the race. His effort is measured out and deep lung-fulls of air are inhaled. He knows that he has a long way to run; his breathing must be controlled. The Olympic high jumper stands on the runway composing herself. She knows that her jump is very technically demanding. She rehearses each step in her mind. She takes a deep breath to enhance her relaxation. She feels composed and starts her approach. The Olympic sprinter has been called to her "marks." Her energy is of excitable calmness. She knows that she needs to be relaxed in her technique but highly energised so as to focus an intense burst of effort. She takes quick, invigorating breaths and waits for the gun to release her down the track.

It almost goes without saying that breathing is a critical part of sporting performance (and of course, life!). It is an autonomic function—it happens without us thinking about it, and yet we can exert some influence over the way it works. Although different sports use a variety of techniques to use breathing to facilitate their performance; it is perhaps surprising that many athletes have poorly developed breathing patterns that actually hinder their performance. I knew a runner who would start to hold is breath when the race tactics changed in a way that he didn't anticipate. Another athlete would take short, shallow breaths—and start to hyperventilate—as soon as she heard her aggressive parents barking instructions from the side of the track. Simply put, breathing patterns can either greatly enhance or hinder a performance.

Before choosing a breathing technique to incorporate into your training decide what is its intended outcome. Some techniques are designed to energise the athlete, other techniques are used for pain control (some of which are used extensively in child-birth.) There are techniques to instill deep relaxation and techniques that enhance concentration.

Breathing is part of the bodies purification system—it removes poisonous waste products (carbon dioxide) and brings oxygen into the blood stream which is then distributed to the tissues and organs. Thus, it has both restorative and invigorating properties; here are some of the techniques that promote such qualities:

Tension –releasing technique

If you have ever attended an opera you have probably been amazed at the power and resonance of the singers voices. These performers will tell you that although their vocal chords shape sound, the volume comes from the use of controlled their breaths and the correct use of their diaphragm. Try this to release tension and enhance relaxation: Find a place that is quiet and where there will be no disruptions. Rest your hands over your abdomen (above the belly-button) so that the tips of several fingers touch. Inhale deeply, this should take 3/ seconds and be slow and controlled. If you are using your diaphragm correctly, your finger tips should gently separate. Let the breath out as slowly as you inhaled. Repeat this process 10 times. Try to empty your mind of any "clutter"—let go of the things that are bothering you.

Quieting response

This is a technique that uses verbal self suggestion in combination with relaxation. On inhaling the athlete makes assertive statements like "I am calm". When exhaling the athlete imagines the breath travelling down the inside of his/her body. This process is repeated three times. This technique is a good one to use in the last few minutes immediately prior to the start of a competition

Breathing for relaxation

The three-part breathing programme is a technique that can help to induce a state of relaxation. After taking a deep diaphragmatic breath the athlete visualises three portions of the lungs, lower, middle, and upper, sequentially filling each with air. This exercise is repeated 3-4 times.

The "5:1 count" is where the athlete takes a large breath and then slowly exhales, this breath is termed number 5. After again inhaling and exhaling the athlete states "I am more relaxed than number 5". The second breath is labelled number 4. And so the process continues so that by number 1 the athlete is more calm and relaxed.

The "1:2 ratio" is a technique where the athlete will inhale for the count of four. On exhalation the athlete counts to eight. This technique is repeated until the athlete reaches a deep and relaxed state.

Breathing for invigoration

There are occasions when athletes need to switch states—from deep relaxation to a more energised approach; early morning training runs is a good example of this. Breath in and out rapidly through the nose but make sure that you keep your mouth tightly shut (thus avoiding hyperventilation). Keep the breaths equal and short. Continue this process for about 30 seconds then stop. With practise, you should find that this technique fills you with energy and heightens your state of preparation.

Breathing for pain control

One technique that, with lots of practise, is particularly effective for pain control is one that combines attention focusing strategies with controlled breathing. Concentrating on the sensations of breath moving in /
out of the nose and mouth can help to shift the focus away from
exercise discomfort (or pain). Having an external focal point—i.e.
a landmark in the race, and alternating that with a focus on relaxed abdominal breaths can also reduce the perception of discomfort.

The athlete may prefer to combine their breathing skills with an internal focal point—i.e. thinking a time and a place (or race) when their breathing and performance seemed to be perfectly in synch. The breathing patterns in a race situation should include controlled, deep invigorating inhalations and exhalations.

Whatever your intended use for these breathing techniques, remember to keep it natural and unstrained. Breathing patterns that are not comfortable for a runner will not be particularly effective.

Jet Lag and Running

You are preparing for one of those sports tourism events and you have chosen the Los Angeles marathon. After months of training you arrive at Heathrow airport full of energy and excitement. The thought of a personal best run teases your muscles throughout the journey. Arriving in California, however, you are absolutely exhausted. The flight has been too long, the seats cramped, and you feel horribly dehydrated. If you think you are tired now, just wait, within a few hours you will find yourself awake in the middle of the night and in the deep fog of fatigue in the day.

Welcome to the world of Jet-Lag!

Leaving London you are living on a Greenwich Mean Time (GMT) body clock. Your body knows when to get tired and when to feel awake. But as you travel across the Atlantic Ocean, the airplane starts to move through numerous time zones. Los Angeles is on Pacific Standard Time (PST) and is 8 hours behind London. Thus, you could leave London at Noon, fly for 10 hours but arrive in LA at 2 p.m. A few hours later your body is saying "it's Midnight and I want to sleep," but the local time is only 4 p.m. Chronobiologists term this phenomenon a "Phase Delay," and it is always associated with westward travel.

Travelling Eastward is known as a "Phase Advance." This is where you might leave Heathrow at 6 p.m., arrive at Moscow after a 3 hour journey but find that it is Midnight. To sleep on "Moscow time," you have to force yourself to sleep even though you feel quite awake.

How does our body create Jet-Lag?

Jet-lag is also known as a circadian rhythm disturbance; a disruption in the sleep-wake cycle. Circadian rhythms are controlled by a section of the brain known as the suprachiasmatic nucleus (SCN). This structure, which is akin to a biological clock, is located in the hypothalamus. Optic nerves cross this structure and this is key in helping the SCN decide whether to instruct the pineal gland to release melatonin. Melatonin is a hormone that causes drowsiness and helps to induce sleep. Light suppresses melatonin production while darkness stimulates its release. Melatonin, while not readily available in the UK, is an over the counter supplement in the United States and is widely used by pilots and international travellers to help them cope with jet-lag.

Jet lag presents itself in the form of increased fatigue, disturbed sleep, decreased mental function and irregular digestive patterns. Other bodily functions also can occur at irregular times—this is a polite way of saying that you can get caught short in the middle of a training run, or worse, a race! Despite these debilitating symptoms, it is not clear is whether jet lag actually leads to a decrement in performance. I once had a race in New Zealand, one day after a 30 hour journey, where I ran to within 1 second of my 800m personal best. Yes, I was jet lagged but my performance didn't seem to suffer. It is possible, however, that a marathon runner would notice the effects of jet lag. Over 800m the symptoms might be understated and overruled by determination, but over extended distances these effects could be amplified; it's best that you have a plan to combat jet-lag.

Ways to cope with jet lag

- The current thinking is that an athlete needs one day to fully adjust for every hour of time change. Thus a runner competing in that Los Angeles race might require 7/8 days to re-synchronize their sleep pattern with local daylight. What can you do if you cannot arrive at the race 3 / 4 days in advance? One technique is to stay up one hour later each day in the few days before you travel, thus easing the adaptive stress on the body.

- Some runners don't adjust their sleeping patterns when they cross various time zones. They stay on their local time zone for sleeping and eating.

- A more sophisticated technique to cope with jet-lag was suggested by Dr. Ehret at Illinois University. Ehret's work concentrated on the role of Zeitgebers—time cues that can shift the runner's body rhythms. Ehret suggested that the timing and nutritional composition of meals can disturb sleep cycles and that these can be used to help an athlete stay awake (phase delay) or fall asleep (in phase advance). Periods of light activity and the use of stimulants (tea, coffee,) can be also used to help the runner make the adjustment in a phase delay.

- Dietary manipulation can limit the effects of jet-lag. Ehret suggested that a high protein breakfast to help stimulate alertness, a high protein lunch and a high carbohydrate dinner (all eaten at local time) will help the athlete make a smooth transition to the new time zone.

- If you have decided that you are going to fully adjust to the new time zone, On arrival at your destination, immediately set your watch to local time. Even though you are exhausted, stay up as long as possible and then try to go to bed at your usual time. If you immediately sleep on arrival, you will be awake throughout the night and it will take you many more days to make the adjustment.

- Avoid alcohol as it can disturb your sleep pattern.

- Sleep in a dark room, or put on those blinds that can be purchased at airports. The darkness is needed for melatonin production.

With all the hard training that you have done it would be a shame to lose its benefits because you did not anticipate or have a plan for the effects of jet-lag. Using these techniques will not only be effective in reducing the effects of this travellers curse, but will also help you to achieve the performance your hard work has earned.

Resolve to be different!
New Year's resolutions and running

The hands of Big Ben edged ever closer to midnight and millions of people across the land charged their glasses with champagne in anticipation of that raucous moment. The festive season had wreaked its havoc on your training plans but your coach said that this was supposed to be "down time," and so you dismissed any guilty thoughts. The crowd of revelers at the party started chanting: "ten, nine, eight.." You raised your glass upward and in doing so, stretched your shirt over the belly that had thickened steadily over the holidays. "Seven, six, five…" The buttons on your shirt, desperately straining to hold you in, finally surrendered to the pressure. "Two, one…Happy New…" Your shirt flew open and sent the offending buttons flying in a glorious arc across the dessert table and into the punch. A couple inches of beer-belly spilled over the edge of your trousers. Horrified, you tucked yourself back-in, but in your mind you were already scribbling a memo in big, black, bold letters: 2005 = Get fit and lose weight!

Much has been written about the power of New Years resolutions. For some they are a tiresome ritual that must be proclaimed with the gusto of a town crier to appreciative family members. Secretly, everybody knows only too well that you are not prepared to bring the energy or conviction to see this resolution through to its completion. Some other people view a resolution as the opportunity to take their life in a new direction, either by the scruff-of the-neck to sort themselves out, or by a planning a modest series of achievable goals.

Sadly, the vast majority of people will fail to complete their stated resolution. One of the reasons is that so many of these declarations immediately demand perfection. They deal with absolutes: You have either kept to your resolution or you have failed. They fail to acknowledge that many of these "bad habits" have been acquired over many months (possibly years). To expect them to change without some kind of transition period is just not realistic.

Making real change, adjusting negative attitudes, conquering harmful habits, can be a messy business. Mistakes are made. "*To err, is to be human,*" but it seems that repeated lapses into "weakness" is enough to de-rail us completely.

These perfect resolutions almost deliberately seek to deny us this aspect of our humanity.

Runners—especially those recently introduced to the sport—are no strangers to these issues. Many fully understand the battles with self-image, the siren call of sugary foods, the pull of easy escape routes when training or racing becomes difficult. Is it a lack of will-power that ultimately defeats us? When in abundance, is this that quality that helps spur other runners to success?

Will power is an attitude and is developed in our habits. Once a month I will choose something that I like to do / eat and then deny myself that pleasure for the sole purpose of enhancing will-power. When faced with running challenges I imagine that I have a fully charged battery of this "fuel" to draw on. It has no mystery ingredients but is formulated with a blend of careful goal-setting (planning), positive attitudes, and a healthy serving of pragmatism. Each day that passes with success adds an extra charge to the battery. The goals that a runner sets should factor-in the ever-changing demands that our complicated lives seem to throw at us. It is okay to state: "*I am going to run every day this month.*" It is a specific and realistic goal. However, a cold, sore throat or a sudden work commitment that requires you to take a few days rest does not equate to the failure of your resolution. Will power is stubborn, but it should also be practical and pliable.

Adjusting entrenched attitudes is difficult. Many of our attitudes have emerged out of experience. Neophyte runners especially those who have always found it to be difficult, may have a collection of unpleasant memories that colour their enjoyment of the experience. Perhaps you repeatedly finished last in the school cross country races. Or maybe you have failed to lose pregnancy weight and have become self-conscious about running in public. Taking part is a courageous first step in adjusting feelings or attitudes and is a sign of strength and commitment toward change. But in times of stress or weakness we often turn back to our old habits for comfort. This is particularly prevalent in people battling addictions (smoking, etc).

Developing new attitudes, whether it is a sustained commitment to an exercise regime, or a more health conscious approach to life can be achieved when the athlete surrounds themselves with like-minded people. So, to give your resolution a fighting chance and join a running club.

This year, I am listening with a keen ear for those bold enough to declare their New Year's resolutions. But as I celebrate with friends and family I'm also going to keep a watchful eye for things floating in the punch!

In the 1970's a runner charged onto the athletic stage with all of the passion and character of a Shakespearean actor. Drama, controversy, and tragedy infused every step of his life. He was a colorful and intriguing character brooking no nonsense on the track and courting controversy with his principled stands against the sporting administration. His name became synonymous with gutsy, hard-faced running; he was:

Steve Prefontaine—A Shooting Star on the track

The life of American Steve Prefontaine is possibly one of the most fabled tales in running-lore. His is the story of an athlete with great talent; a man with strong opinions and an athlete with an unyielding attitude towards pain. With his trademark front running, full of hubris, Prefontaine lit up the track and burned his rivals with some of the most aggressive and awe-inspiring front running the world has ever seen. Those already familiar with his life, know that this story does not have a happy ending. Pre—as he was known—was killed in a car accident aged 24, his potential clearly unfilled. His life has been the subject of two recent Hollywood films, countless books and articles. His name is honoured in one of track's great annual meetings: The Prefontaine Classic held in Eugene, Oregon.

So why write about this man and his achievements now? Is there anything left to say that hasn't already been said before? This account is more than a story of a man and his races, his successes and defeats. Here we will attempt to understand the mind of one of the toughest and most determined runners to leave a mark in track legend. There is no better way to reflect on this runner's contribution, to understand his approach to running, maybe even glimpse into the complex mind of a champion athlete, than by using his own words:

"To give anything less than your best is to sacrifice the gift." Steve Prefontaine understood that running to your potential requires more than a vague commitment to training. Anyone can say that they are prepared to work hard and reap the rewards of hard training. It takes a tough leathery hide to take a beating session after session, to face a fierce wind and not let it break your spirit, and most important, to not let a setback limit your future performances. Prefontaine recognised that his talent was extraordinary and would take him to amazing places; it was something that he was not going to take for granted.

Motivation is a pillar of a successful athlete's achievement. Runners will have to ask themselves the question "what motivates me to be the best?" The answers are not always easy to find. The hardships and solace of a runner's pursuit of excellence carry a personal price and it is not something that all runners are prepared to pay. Prefontaine understood this inner turmoil and used it to his advantage: "You have to wonder at times what you're doing out there. Over the years, I've given myself a thousand reasons to keep running, but it always comes back to where it started. It comes down to self-satisfaction and a sense of achievement."

He recognised that there was a certain artistry and drama in running. "Some people create with words or with music or with a brush and paints. I like to make something beautiful when I run. I like to make people stop and say, 'I've never seen anyone run like that before.' It's more than just a race, it's a style. It's doing something better than anyone else. It's being creative."

In 1972 Prefontaine found himself in Munich, Germany for the Olympic Games: an event that was painfully scarred by a terrorist attack that killed 11 Israeli athletes. Preparing to race in the 5000m, Prefontaine, like many games participants, found himself searching for answers and meaning to this appalling tragedy. It was to have a deep and draining effect on the young athlete from Coos Bay, Oregon; but somehow, he realised that he would have overcome his emotional fatigue and run like he had never run before.

Pre's main rival at the games would be the Finn, Lasse Viren, a stalk-like runner whose long easy strides contrasted the muscular frame of Prefontaine. Viren was blessed with incredible leg speed and had honed his endurance with months of 100—150 miles per week. He had already won the 10,000m in a world record time and exuded a frightening presence on the track.

Pre had shown himself to be adept at front-running, at surging, at fiercely changing pace, but would he have the finishing speed to drop the predatory Finn? Heading into the race Prefontaine issued a clear statement of his intent: *"Somebody may beat me, but they are going to have to bleed to do it." "A lot of people run a race to see who is fastest. I run to see who has the most guts, who can punish himself into exhausting pace, and then at the end, punish himself even more. Nobody is going to win a 5,000 meter race after running an easy 2 miles. Not with me. If I lose forcing the pace all the way, well, at least I can live with myself."*

Many pundits expected Pre to charge straight to the front and unleash a ruthless exhibition of front running. This, they thought, would be a race of attrition with nobody in contention in the final charge for the medals. To everyone's surprise the pace in the early stages was pedestrian with every runner in the field able to take a turn at the front. Prefontaine found himself boxed in, that classic tactical conundrum: being able to run much faster, but being unable to find a way to pass the runners surrounding you. Observers could feel Prefontaine's discomfort, like a train with a full head of steam he was bursting to find a track to the front. Lap after lap clicked by and Viren, Ian Stewart of England, Mohammed Gamoudi from Morroco jockeyed for pole position. With four laps to go a gap finally opened and Pre saw his chance. The crowd roared as if an electrical charge had just shot out of this pack of runners; our front-runner was free!

There is a conventional wisdom in track running that if you wish to break the spirit and drain the speed of a fast finishing rival, you must do so by raising the pace to a level that your rival cannot sustain. With four laps remaining Pre surged hard and held that pace, a 62 second lap. The next lap was faster still at 61 seconds. Most runners would have wilted under such a withering pace, but Viren clung to the heels of the American like a limpet refusing to yield to the pressure of a wave. Viren then charged into the lead injecting a 60 second lap and stating his clear desire to claim another gold. Entering into the final lap Viren, Pre, Stewart and the Morrocan, Gamoudi, lined up to deliver their final sprint; the strain showed on each runners face; it was that seminal moment that Prefontaine had spoken about, he was going to see who had the most guts! Tearing down the back straight, Pre maneuvered himself to pass Viren. Each athlete was now sprinting as hard as they could. Viren refused to yield. Gamoudi pulled alongside Prefontaine and impeded the American's attempt to get past Viren. Into the finishing straight Viren forced himself towards the line, desperate to hold off one final charge from the exhausted American and the inspired Morrocan.

Having given his absolute best effort, Prefontaine stumbled in the final three metres and was passed by Ian Stewart. He was out of the medals. Incredibly, and showing how fast running had progressed in the 18 years since Roger Bannisters record breaking run, Steve Prefontaine had run his last mile of this

5000m in just a touch over 4 four minutes!

Prefontaine was emotionally drained from Munich and returned to his beloved Oregon in search of recovery. Never one to soberly reflect on a setback, Pre set his sights towards Montreal, Canada, home of the next Olympic Games (1976). Tragically, he would not live to race Viren again; his death robbing the sport of one of the most colorful, determined, and inspiring athletes to race on the international stage.

Lasse Viren faded into relative obscurity between the Munich and Montreal Olympics. However, on his return, he stunned the distance running world by claiming both the 5000 and 10,000 metre titles again. The press rightly hailed Viren as the greatest distance runner in Olympic history; but one can't help wonder what role a young American from Coos Bay would have played in those races.

Shooting stars may burn out fast, but they are glorious to watch and we always remember them.

Shooting Star! The life and running of Steve Prefontaine.

Three cheers for that runner! Hip-hip...
(How crowds effect your performance)

The crowd that had assembled at Crystal Palace Stadium, August 30th 1982, knew that something special was about to happen. A brilliant afternoon of athletics had thrilled an appreciative crowd, but there was a clear sense that the best race was yet to come. The final event of the day was the 4 by 800m relay race and Great Britain had assembled a team of almost unparalled talent and achievement: Sebastian Coe, Steve Cram, Peter Elliot and Gary Cook; a group with a cluster of world records and Olympic medals to their names. A nation feasting on a diet of world distance running records now set its voracious appetite for the world 4x800m record.

As an 18 year old invited to run for the Great Britain "C" team, this was a dream come to true. I would run the last leg for my team and would measure up against Sebastian Coe. Even though he was 9 seconds faster than me (a huge distance over 800m) I decided to give him a run for his money (which I'm sure was more than the 20 pounds I received for my travelling expenses...however, I digress!).

The first leg was run by Peter Elliot—a man destined to be an Olympic medallist and world record holder (indoors). Although he was rusty from 3 weeks holiday, Elliot took the "A" team into a commanding lead. He passed the baton over to Garry Cook—an Olympic silver medallist in the 4x400m relay—and also a brilliant 800m runner. Cook ran a determined leg and built an unassailable lead over my team, Great Britain "C". The third leg saw Steve Cram greedily consume the track with his giant strides, he ran a stunning 1m 44 second split in what was essentially a time trial.

20,000 people in the stadium, and probably millions more watching on television, leapt to their feet. The "A" team was well ahead of the world record schedule and Sebastian Coe was about to take over. Breaking the record seemed a certainty. The excitement of the crowd built the noise to an ear splitting level and it was hard to control the adrenaline fizzing through my veins.

I can now understand how people can make profound errors in sport (and life) when their excitement level peaks, then over-flows. Coe sprinted off and went through 400m in a touch under 50 seconds. Even though he was completely out of sight, I too sprinted off in pursuit and went through 400m in well under 50 seconds. The crowd was now screaming as Coe raced through 600m, 700m. He didn't seem to tire. I raced through 500, 600m feeling great but then my body took great offence at the way that I was treating it. Suddenly my legs refused to support the weight of the rest of my body; any pretensions I had of gazelle-like grace disappeared as I started to stagger towards the finishing line. Meanwhile Coe had sprinted across the line helping his team to shatter the world record.

There are some mistakes that are made in a running race that can be corrected. A tactical error, followed by an adjustment, is in the natural course of a race. But some mistakes—especially in pacing—can be unforgiving. If you set your pace too fast, you may end up in a corner of Crystal Palace Stadium violently throwing up while Coe and Cram are busy accepting the applause from the crowd! Ahh, when gods and mere mortals clash on the track.

I would have never set off at such a suicidal pace in any other race, so why did I throw all restraint away on that day? Was I too caught up in the moment? What made me think that as an 18 year old I could match, if not beat, the pace of the world's greatest runners? Was it arrogance, immaturity, or a just a mistake?

Social Facilitation

The answer may be found with an understanding of the principle known in psychology as social facilitation. In 1898, the psychologist Norman Triplett noted that people in bicycle races went faster when they were competing against each other directly than when they were racing in an individual time trial. He theorised that the presence of others enhanced performance. Decades later, Robert Zajonc expanded this idea and suggested that performance was linked to the state of arousal. He suggested that tension, excitement and anxiety were possible responses when an athlete was asked to perform in a situation (i.e. a race). An athlete used to racing in front of 20,000 spectators (like Coe, Cram) would probably have controlled excitement, something that Zajonc termed: the dominant response. These athletes had learned how to use the crowd's enthusiasm to their advantage. For less experienced runners, an easy task would be performed better when others were around. However, complex or unfamiliar tasks (e.g. performing in-front of large crowds) may create anxiety, or uncontrolled excitement, and cause you to make mistakes.

While the support offered to thousands runners is a welcomed boost, especially in marathons, voluminous cheering can also have a negative effect on the ill-disciplined athlete. The presence of others at a race or training session may effect us in a number of ways:

- The cheering crowd can raise our adrenaline levels and while this may elevate performance for awhile, it can also cause runners to make errors if unchecked. Sudden bursts of speed, in response to this encouragement, may actually break the rhythm and tempo of the runner and be counter-productive. This boost may be helpful at the end of the race, but the last thing you need mid-way through the London marathon is to start sprinting! Accept the encouragement but keep your responses under control.

- No-one wants to look terrible in-front of a crowd. We would like to be seen as fit and fluent; an impressive athlete in command of our body. However, a fear of being judged by others can increase our arousal and also push us into tactics or pacing strategies that are not self-serving.

- Excessive cheering from the crowd can also distract an inexperienced athlete to the point where they actually stop performing. Focusing on technique, energy conservation, breathing patterns, evaluating your tactics, can all serve to enhance the athlete's concentration.

It has been 22 years since that sunny August day but my memory of that day will never fade. Those runners were truly amazing, and the record? It still stands.

Running has long been a chauvinistic sport and a traditional view was that women were not meant to be distance runners. In the 1970's the longest distance a women could race on the track was 1500m. One sports administrator in England was heard complaining that young girls should not be allowed to run long distances for seeing them out of breath was both unsettling and un-lady like.

For a social attitudes to change, sometimes it requires and influential, if not charismatic force to convince the world that the change should be embraced. The story you are about to read is of a young lady who showed the world that women could run long distances with grace and determination. Women wanted change and Grete Waitz was, inadvertently, going to lead them...

The Heart of the New York Marathon: The Grete Waitz story

In the 1970's a young girl from Norway started to make her mark in the world of running. Grete Andersen was tall, skinny, and held her hair in pigtails that bounced with each of her loping strides. Like many Norwegians, she spent much of her winter on cross country skis and as a teenager it was obvious that she had an incredible capacity for aerobic activity. She took up running and within a few years Grete was ranked first in the world at 1500 and 3000 meters. You would think that she was blessed with impressive speed, but Grete Andersen (soon to marry Jack Waitz) was a strength runner and her lack of raw speed was found to be lacking at the 1976 Montreal Olympic Games. Heavily favoured to take an Olympic title, Grete failed to reach the final of the 1500m, which at that time was the longest event a woman could race at the games.

Shifting her attention to more endurance oriented events, Grete won five world cross-country titles. She then set world records in the five-mile, 10K, 15K, 20K, and ten-mile events. But success on the track seemed to elude her; quite simply the events were not long enough. By 1978, Grete had had enough of running. She had always tried to fit her hard training around her career as an elementary school teacher, but it seemed that her enjoyment of this had left her. Her typical day was starting at 5 a.m. with a training run, putting in a long day with her students, then running again at night. She had been a blazing star in the track world but now she was burning out.

In November, 1978 events transpired that were to take her life in a new and unexpected direction. Grete decided that she would like to try the marathon; one final race before retirement. An invitation from Fred Lebow, the New York Road Runners Club president and race director, asked Grete to set the pace for the more serious runners. She agreed to run and on race day felt full of energy. With no expectations on her, Grete launched herself into the race almost with reckless abandon. Her longest training run in preparation for the event had been 12 miles but she had a deep well of aerobic conditioning, born from winters spent on the ski trails, upon which she could draw.

The first twenty miles clicked by with ease and Grete established a significant lead. Then she started to suffer, *"I just kept thinking, when is this going to end?"* She struggled through intense cramp and just made it across the finish line, her time: A new world record, 2 hours 32 minutes and 29 seconds. Not bad for a lady planning to retire!

That famous Autumn day was the start of what was to be a long term love affair with the New York Marathon. Grete Waitz was to win this race 9 times and would break the world record a total of four times.

In 1983, Grete finally won a world championship (other than the cross country title) when she won the inaugural women's marathon championship. Her plans now focused on the Los Angeles Olympics, which, in all likelihood, would probably represent her last chance of claiming that elusive gold medal. It was expected that the heat of a LA summer would stifle endurance performances and all runners would have to race with caution and respect for the conditions. The pace early in the race was sedentary and Waitz held back. A seemingly more reckless runner named Joan Benoit sprang into an early lead and stated her intention to run away with the race. May good fortune favour the foolish, and upon such risks races can be decided. That day, an unusual cool air mass swept in off the Pacific, and too everyone's surprise the thermometer did not rise as anticipated. Rather than seeing her rival struggle in the heat, Waitz had let Benoit build up an unassailable lead. Benoit's victory was on the of the great surprises of the games, but Grete's silver medal was a just reward for a lady that had dominated running for at least 14 years.

Grete Waitz was responsible for showing the world that not only could women run long distances, but they could run fast times and beat many men. Her last world record, 2 hours: 25 minutes 28 seconds would still give her a high placing in today's New York marathon.

Grete Waitz: The Heart of the New York Marathon!

Getting back to basics: The simplicity of running

Everybody enjoys a successful racing or training experience. Some times these experiences come after careful planning and are the realisation of a life long dream. There are also occasions when the performance was an unexpected lightning flash of brilliance—something that you may never repeat. The thrill of personal success is very rewarding and can propel us to ever-tougher training regimes. It can re-invigorate our mental and physical energies and help us to aim for an even higher level of performance.

It would be wonderful if we could reproduce these experiences on demand but there are times when we just have to accept that it is just not our day. Acceptance of a sub-standard performance is not something that comes easily for an athlete, nor should it. Striving for one's best should also be accompanied by a disatisfaction with anything less than that ideal. I am more concerned with athletes whom don't seem to care what happens rather than the athlete who beats themselves up after a bad race.

The very nature of the sport requires the athlete to constantly analyse their effort, their energy distribution (pacing, etc), and their technique. This analysis is the feedback component that allows us to correct our mistakes, adjust our training, and re-evaluate our goals. The question that inevitably resonates through your search for improvement is "*where did I go wrong?*" You may decide to take advice from experts but this could be confusing; one coach might extol the benefits of high mileage, another stressing the importance of intervals. Has your training been wrong? You now have a wealth of information at your fingertips: journals, magazines, internet chatlines, but sorting the kernel from the chafe requires skill. The phrase
"*A little knowledge is a dangerous thing*" is a cautionary reminder that no every piece of training wisdom is well conceived or suitable for you.

You seem to have more questions than answers: Which training technique should have the greatest emphasis in your training? Intervals, aerobic conditioning, or anaerobic threshold training? Should you rely on your natural talent or work tirelessly on your technique? Should you read and try to copy the training logs of successful athletes?

You understand that training and coaching has never been a precise science and that a one size fits all training methodology does not suit you.

Pretty soon your head is whirring with ideas and rather than finding a path to improvement, you are actually lacking direction. Sports psychologists might suggest that you are in a state of *"analysis—paralysis."*

Attention to detail in race preparation has often been associated with the professionalism of an elite athlete. They have an action plan for the race, alternative strategies if the race unfolds in an unexpected way, a plan to pull out all their resources of hard training. The danger in over-analysing every single possible risk, benefit, tactic, counter tactic, etc, is that you can actually stop competing. You become too busy thinking and not concentrating on "doing-it." The phrase *"The Devil is in the details,"* can be counter-intuitive in athletic performance. It may be tempting to plan for every eventuality—believing that you can bring all aspects of the race and your performance under your control, but the reality is that this never happens.

Rather than being a source of comfort and confidence, I knew an athlete whom became anxious when there was variance in one of the race details that he thought he controlled. The logic should be that every athlete would like to control the race why should your plan be the infallible one? Interviews with successful athletes revealed that they understand that any race plan is a fluid set of constructs moulded around ever-changing conditions.

So how do you find direction when your mind seems so unsure as to where to go? The locker-room *"Keep it simple stupid"* (the KISS approach) is a crass reminder that our sport is fundamentally a natural expression of movement. It is play and is meant to be fun. Children understand the simplicity of play and don't need complicated rules to dictate its flow. As adults we easily lose our way by examining, analyzing, trying to synthesise massive amounts of information in the hope that it will make us a better athlete. It almost seems paradoxical that an athlete can often improve by returning to simplicity; *"getting back to basics"* as it is known in the vernacular. Albert Schweitzer, the great humanitarian and scientist, once wrote: *"We move from naïve simplicity to profound simplicity."* Certainly you should use your knowledge of training to help guide you on your path to improved performances, but emphasise the simplicity of it all. Have fun, stop worrying about details and outcome. Have Fun (it's worth repeating) and enjoy your inevitable return to form.

Every runner can have a bad day. Too often, and to our detriment, we reflect on that performance with condemnatory angst. We feel every ounce of strain, curse every stinging bead of sweat, grimace through each aching step towards disappointment and the finishing line. We forget our previous successes and live in this frustrating moment as if we had never experienced anything else but this sorry state of mind.

This next story is not about failure…it is a celebration of the successes of one of the greatest marathon runners in history. But at what should have been a highlight in a brilliant career this runner suffered a sensational collapse in front of millions of shocked television viewers. His story is about the triumph of the human spirit but it doesn't follow the kind of timeline associated with a Hollywood film script (our hero clinches success in the final stride, etc). This runner needed several years of healing before he could return to finish his final race. The story here is simple but the message powerful: Even if you can't get up and finish the race today, still try to get up and finish it tomorrow, or next month or next year. May you remind yourself of your previous successes, move past the difficult period in your life, and allow your spirit to truly soar…

Finishing the Final Lap: The Jim Peters Story

I want you to imagine this: You have gathered in an Olympic Stadium to watch Sebastian Coe and Steve Ovett battle over 1500m. The pre-race hype fills the airwaves and covers the front pages of every newspaper. The race is as exciting and dramatic as any that you have ever seen. 20 minutes later you await the arrival of Paula Radcliffe in the women's marathon. She has a massive lead— perhaps 15 minutes—and the gold medal is a certainty; all she has to do is enter the stadium and jog a lap of the track. Instead, what you see is deeply shocking; she staggers into the stadium and then falls on the track. She pulls herself up very slowly and resumes running. She falls again, and again. All sense of coordination has fled her body. The stadium is silent. Somebody help her! She is lifted off the track and fails to complete the race.

As the weeks pass sporting history focuses on her valiant attempts on that infamous last lap. All but forgotten are her magnificent world records, her championship medals, her contributions to our sport. This is a terrible injustice that the media will fail to correct for the rest of her sporting career. She was the athlete that fell, not the athlete that ran. Is this fictional tale unrealistic?

Skip back 50 years.

You have just finished watching "The Miracle Mile," and the atmosphere in the stadium is electric. Bannister has defeated Landy and both men have run under four minutes for the mile. Does sport get any better than this you ask? Soon the marathon runners will enter the stadium, this will be a fitting end to a spectacular sports festival (The Empire Games). Jim Peters of England has an unassailable lead—estimated to be at least 3 miles over his nearest rival. But something is wrong......

Our story starts in Dagenham, Essex. Like many young boys in the 1930's Jim Peters had a keen interest in sports which he developed when he joined the Dagenham Boys Club. Soon he displayed a talent for running. Even though he would run races in his house slippers (he couldn't afford to buy spikes), he set county records on the track. Within a few years he was the British 6 mile champion. When turning 30, most runners in the modern era would probably believe that their best years are behind them. Not so, for Jim Peters. He was just getting started.

After years of developing his strength in cross country and distance racing, he turned his hand to marathon running. This event was a natural fit for the optician with a slender physique. At a time when rest, light training, and moderation were key principles of training, Jim Peters brought a determined, almost brusque attitude to his race preparations. He did not believe in easy running. In his autobiography he stated "the body has to be conditioned to stand up to the stresses and strains which it is going to met in a race."

In 1952, Jim smashed the world marathon record with a time of 2hours 25:39. He headed into the 1952 Helsinki Olympic Games as the obvious favourite but would face an amazing runner from Czechoslovakia: Emile Zatopek. Zatopek had just won the Olympic 5000m and 10,000m titles; his trademark crunched shoulders and distorted expressions of fatigue masked the ease with which he ran. He fixed his sights on the marathon title and a clash with Jim Peters.

Peters was brimming with confidence and laid out the challenge for Zatopek. With aggressive front running, Peters quickly established a 16 second lead at 10km, but by 25km he seemed to be struggling. The first of a series of intense cramps were rippling through his body. Zatopek moved alongside; this was his first marathon and he was unsure of the pace. He turned to Peters and asked "are we going fast enough?" Peters' cheeky response suggested that Zatopek would have to run much faster than this pace to beat him. Zatopek promptly changed gears and ran away from Peters! The Czech became the only runner in Olympic history to claim 3 distance running titles at the same games. Jim was forced out of the race at the 30km, he would have to focus his training towards another race.

Today, the London Marathon has grown into an enormous cultural and sporting festival, but for many years—before marathon running became popular—the closest the capital came to its own race was the Polytechnic Marathon. This race weaved its way around West London and finished in Chiswick stadium. Fueled by his disappointment in Helsinki, Peters was determined to prove that he—and not Zatopek—was the fastest marathon runner in the world. He stamped his authority on the race and finished in 2hours 20:42; a new world record by almost five minutes.

Applying his personal motto: "Train little, hard and often," Jim prepared to take the marathon to a new level. In 1953 he became the first person to run under 2hours 20minutes as he recorded 2:18.40, again at the Polytechnic Marathon. The next year he repeated his record breaking feat by running an amazing 2:17.39.

Four world records in four years; a remarkable achievement that was recognised when the IAAF (International Amateur Athletic Federation) identified Jim as one of the three best marathon runners of all-time (along side Abebe Bikila of Ethiopea and Carlos Lopes of Portugal).

In 1954 Jim had the chance to add an international championship title to his achievements as The Empire Games were held in Vancouver, Canada. Race day was scorching hot (86 degrees in the shade) and the 16 runners that lined up at the start were to face challenging conditions. Dehydration quickly effected the runners—one athlete, Stan Cox, ran into a telegraph pole and knocked himself out. Peters ran at great speed seemingly in defiance of the conditions. He took no water and did not let up on his torrid pace, even though he had established a huge lead.

By the time Jim entered the stadium, his body had overheated, it was dehydrated and he was in a state of near collapse. He kept falling to the track but such was the man's courage and determination that he pulled himself up, again and again. With 200m left to run Jim Peters collapsed and was rendered assistance by team managers (incidentally, Dr. Roger Bannister, fresh from his victory in the Miracle Mile just minutes earlier, administered medical treatment). This was a heart wrenching experience for the athlete and the crowd that willed him to finish. Such was the trauma that Jim Peters retired from running soon after. With cruel irony it was later suggested that the course was 27 miles long and Jim had in fact successfully completed the marathon distance.

There was, however, a delightful turn of events. Jim Peters was held with such great affection with the people of Vancouver that several years later he was invited back to complete his final lap around that famous track.
His journey as an athlete was now complete.

In 1979 I had the privilege of meeting the great Jim Peters. I was a young runner and completely ignorant of the man's achievements. Introducing myself I said rather crassly "you were the runner who collapsed on the track." His shoulders dropped and for a moment a tinge of sadness came across his face, he then graciously offered words of encouragement for my running career. This essay is my apology. Jim Peters was more than a man remembered for collapsing, he was more than a man who broke four world records, he was simply Jim Peters: A great runner!

Have you assessed your running machine?

If runners were cars, I guess that I have to face the reality that I do not have the dashing speed of a Ferrari. I do not possess the sleek lines of an Aston Martin; and sadly, when it comes to power and performance, I am more of a beater than Rolls Royce. Once a year all aging vehicles submit themselves for a check-up. A thorough examination of the vehicle's safety and road-worthiness is made and any flaws are corrected.

The Running Machine

It's not uncommon for sports commentators to describe the brilliance of a runner's performance: "*she's absolutely destroying the field, she's a running machine!*" It's an intriguing metaphor for a runner's body is essentially an organic version of a complex piece of machinery. It has energy production systems, a command and control centre (the brain), a pump (the heart), a gas exchange system (the lungs). With training, each system can be challenged to improve its efficiency and functioning. Different types of running can help the energy production systems to improve their operations: e.g. a long run will enhance aerobic efficiency, while fast runs with short recovery will stress the anaerobic energy system. The efficiency of the heart and lungs is also improved with consistent and intense levels of exercise.

A good engine also needs the right fuel prompting the question: Are you eating well? Do your nutritional habits help or hinder your performance?

Part of on-going maintenance is to consider if you need to fine tune any of the machine's components or decide if you need a complete overhaul. Fine tuning for a runner may involve polishing a skill that is need of refreshment; e.g. without practise an athlete can lose the "zip" in their sprint finish. Regular practise of this skill—kicking off different paces—will help this athlete. A complete overhaul maybe necessary if your training and racing has stagnated e.g. if the same training is bringing a declining level of performance. You may need to re-design your training: Are you training enough? Do you push yourself or take it easy?

But what about the brain? Can we improve its functioning?

Train the Brain!

Mental skills present the athlete with opportunities, the chance to utilise latent or known skills in ways that can enhance performance. So the brain thinks, so the body responds. Obviously, the type of training that we give it will shape its effectiveness in command and control decisions over the athlete's body. Repeatedly telling the muscles to relax will bring—with training—the desired response. Repeatedly expressing positive thoughts will help to diminish the harmful effects of negative thinking.

Consider the following checkpoints in your assessment:

• Reflection: Appraise your training and racing

Repeated success, high levels of personal enjoyment and motivation would suggest that your training and racing is on the right track. However, making the same mistakes, no progress, a lack of will power and fun is suggestive of an athlete who needs a fresh approach. Are you self-coached? May be you need the innovative input of a coach.

• Goal Setting

Consider this next phase of your running career as a year-long journey: Where are you going? How long will it take you to reach your destination?
What will make the journey more enjoyable? Are there any diversions along the way? How will you deal with them?

• A review of your personal qualities

Do they help you fulfill your potential or limit your enjoyment? Are you mentally tough or do you prefer the path of least resistance? Set out your "mental skill priorities"— which qualities would you like to exhibit the most. How will you incorporate this desire into an action plan?

So are you a beater (all covered in rust) with dreams of being a Ferrari? Are you *"All revved-up with nowhere to go?"* Then give yourself an assessment and see where the road may take you!

When is this race going to end?

A few strides into the last five miles of her Ironman, Sarah Picard knew she was in trouble. Her reserves of glycogen had long been exhausted and she was running on "fumes." Only the will-power made from hundreds of hours spent on the road prevented her from dropping out. She squinted into the distance in miserable attempt to see the finish line. Each step felt like her last but some how she moved forward; her thoughts of high performance had evaporated with the sweat pouring out of her body, all that remained was the question pounding in her head *"when is this race going to end?"*

Even though a mile is just a mile, it can sometimes have an elastic quality in the minds of a runner. We can make it seem so much shorter when we are full of relaxation, rhythm and running. But we can make it last an eternity when we are struggling. What accounts for this difference in perception?

In the 1970's, Gunnar Borg, a Swedish physiologist, was tasked with finding a means from preventing cardiac rehabilitation patients from over-exerting themselves. Borg developed the "ratings of perceived exertion" (RPE) which with training, helped patients to accurately assess their level of exertion. Borg suggested that the perception of exertion was a "gestalt," a feeling that integrated information from the central nervous system, heart and ventilation rates, and local cues such as blood lactate and muscle temperature.

The Borg Scale

6

7............ Very, very light—this run required almost no effort

8

9............ This was an easy run

10

11............Fairly light—This run did not require too much effort

12

13......Somewhat hard—Although challenging at times, I had plenty left

14

15......... Hard—this was a demanding run

16

17......... Very hard—I could not keep going for much longer

18

19......... very, very hard—I am totally exhausted.

20

Multiplying any number by 10 would give an approximation of the individual's heart rate. Not surprisingly, a competitive athlete will likely have scores from 15—19.

Why is RPE important for an athlete?

Research using the Borg scale suggested that 70% of the "gestalt" (the overall feeling of exertion) is explained by physiological measures with the remainder being drawn from psychological variables. A number of studies found that these scores could be manipulated by an athlete's style of thinking. One technique that was proven to be particularly effective was termed dissociation. Athletes were trained to block their perception of exertion, and to minimise feelings of muscular tension or fatigue by distracting their mind with mundane challenges. Spontaneous thoughts, mental diversions, and problem solving formed the basis of dissociation thoughts. Athletes relying on the dissociation thought technique to help them through difficult patches in their race might get a false reading using the Borg scale. They could under or over exert themselves (an error in pace judgement) and not realise this mistake before it was too late.

The converse of dissociation was termed the Association technique, and here, athletes were trained to concentrate on the physiological information their body was generating and use it to modify their pace and effort. These athletes could use the Borg scale to their benefit.

Feelings of fatigue can be influenced by the expectations of the task's duration. Athletes struggling through the mid-section of a long distance race may find their perception of effort and fatigue varies even though, in reality, both factors have not changed. Ulmer, a sports psychologist, introduced "teleoanticipation" a concept that describes how the effort to reach a certain goal is modified by the athlete's perception of distance left to run. Studies revealed that runners asked to maintain a constant effort saw their work output decline at the middle of the race and then increased at the end. So what? Athletes have known for years about the inspiring magic of the finishing line; it is something that draws out our last reserves and brings us to completion. This study does show, however, that athletes using mental techniques (such as association) during this "slump" stretch of the race may be able to maintain their effort more consistently than

those runners not in tune with their body.

Riggs, an exercise physiologist, has suggested that endorphins (the natural body opiates produced during exercise) may induce a cataleptic state in some runners. This is where the athlete has a reduced responsiveness to stimuli and, allegedly, experiences the suspension of sensation. Athletes training their minds to use the association technique may thus receive a number of benefits connected to perceptions of exertion:

- Improved pace judgement
- Better energy management
- Monitoring of physical stress e.g. overheating, injury prevention
- A greater awareness of what their body is capable of in the midst of a race.

Perseverance and the spirit of not losing

In today's media-blitz world we see the gold medals and the photos of star athletes on news stands. We are attracted to the adulation they receive from the screaming crowds of admirers and it secretly makes us want to join their lap of honour, if not replace them (if only we had their talent!) The lights, the cameras, the celebrity success, this is the modern day sporting hero presented to us in a "greatest hits" package. Scratch away the superficial gloss and you will see a different person. This is the person who is weary from hour after hour of hard work. This is the runner coping with constant soreness and fatigue. There is a solace, maybe loneliness, in their singular pursuit for excellence and it is something that would break the spirit of a less determined athlete.

I want to share with you three stories, each charting an amazing athletic achievement. These are the tales of three very different types of runner, but with one powerful quality that ties them together…

When Roger Bannister burst through the tape, becoming the first human to run under four minutes for one mile, it was more than another world record. This was a performance that showed the world that the range of human potential cannot be restrained by thought; imagining the impossible is often the starting point for achieving the incredible. But there is no guarantee of success no matter how much you want it, and perhaps that is just as well; the greatest thrills of achievement often come when there is also the strong possibility of defeat. Bannister had failed in several attempts to break the record and other athletes, John Landy from Australia and Wes Santee from America, were also closing in on that achievement. What was it in Bannister's character that propelled him to that record?

Battling her way to victory in this year's New York marathon, Paula Radcliffe bravely showed the running world that adversity and set-back can be overcome with determination. Her disappointment at the Athens Olympics could have easily de-railed her season, maybe even her career. It takes a courageous athlete to stare down those demons and chart a path to recovery.

The story of a young man named Terry Fox, may not be known to many of you, but if you live in Canada, he is recognised as a national hero. A bronze statue in his honour stands as a testimony to courage, self-sacrifice and athletic achievement. As a teenager Terry experienced the trauma of cancer and his right leg was amputated 6 inches above the knee. However he loved running and was soon fitted with a prosthetic limb that allowed him to practise.

Those of you who are preparing for a marathon will understand the fatigue that accompanies the hard training. When you finish the race, wrapped-up in those foil blankets, you will probably consider and enjoy the significance of your achievement. Imagine then, setting yourself the goal of running a marathon every day until you run across Canada—the 2ⁿᵈ largest country in the world! Terry Fox decided to call his journey The Marathon of Hope and that he would raise money for cancer research. The fatigue and pain was debilitating as he hobbled in a strange shuffle step, yet the look of determination on his face endeared him to the public.

So what ties these athletes together?

In Japan they have a word, Makenki, which means the spirit of not losing. In Finland they use the word Sisu, meaning, to persevere when all others would quit. In the vernacular we might state: When the going gets tough, the tough get going. It is perseverance that has shaped the character, and thus the achievements, of each of these great athletes. It is a quality that expresses itself through courage, it is the spirit in a determined runner's eyes, it is the defiant refusal to yield when adversity threatens to engulf you. Of course this is not a uniform quality displayed by all hard-working athletes. Some people possess an unrelenting desire to achieve their purpose, no matter what. Others fold in the face of the slightest difficulty. Can perseverance be trained? Consider this quote from the great Czech runner Emil Zatopek *"when a person trains once, nothing happens. When a person forces themselves to do a thing a hundred or a thousand times, then they have developed in more ways than physical…then willpower (and thus, perseverance) will be no problem."*

After running a marathon every day for 143 days and covering 3,300 miles, Terry Fox was forced to stop running because cancer had appeared in his lungs. He could not complete his challenge and he passed away on June 28, 1981 at age 22. Every year, the Terry Fox Run is held across Canada, and in many other countries around the world. Today, the Terry Fox Foundation has raised $360 million for cancer research.

Perseverance has served each of these great athletes well, may it be a lodestone in your running career.

Anxiety and running

Two runners, one race. Each athlete has trained for months with diligence and a clearly stated goal of running well on this day. Their long runs have been blended with speed training and both athletes feel they are ready to perform to a high standard. However a few hours before that start of the race one of the athletes is noticeably agitated. He seems distracted and is talking about what might happen if he performs poorly. As the race start time draws near, he makes frequent visits to the bathroom and complains about being thirsty.

Our other athlete has approached the same race with a calm and composed mind. He has set his thoughts on the race tactics and is focusing on the things that he can control. He prepares for the start with confidence.

So which athlete has a great race? The athlete with the anxiety has a storming run and destroys his equally talented opponent with an aggressive piece of front running. How can this be? For all the sports psychology research that cautions us to fear anxiety, I believe that talent and fitness still has the ability to trump anxiety and some of its debilitating symptoms. I think of anxiety as a shadow force; an energising power that can activate the mind and body, but left unchecked, it can ravage a performance.

What is anxiety and how does it relate to running?

The standard manual for diagnosing psychiatric / psychological conditions (DSM -IV) includes the following symptoms for general anxiety: muscle soreness, trembling, restlessness, fatigue, shortness of breath, tachycardia, sweating, dizziness nausea and vomiting, being on edge, startle response, blank mind, poor sleep and irritability. Anxiety disorders can include anything from simple phobias, to obsessive compulsive disorders. There are many athletes who have had these conditions find expression in harmfully excessive training, obsessive monitoring of nutrition, etc.

As anxiety, and its associated kin, stress, have become a blight of modern day living, it is not surprising that it has attracted the interest of psychologists attempting to further understand its origins, behaviours, and other manners of expression. Spielberger (1966) wrote that anxiety took two main forms: State and trait anxiety. State anxiety was considered to be situational in nature and associated with arousal of the autonomic nervous system. Trait anxiety is a world-view that an individual uses when coping with situations that present themselves to the athlete—i.e. some people are pre-disposed to looking at things with an anxious manner.

Research has revealed that an athlete who is low trait anxious but is experiencing a high condition of state anxiety will find it facilitative to peak performance. Thus, the athlete in our example was probably not someone who was generally anxious but on the race day felt the effects of this condition. Rather than limiting his performance, and counter intuitively, it actually provided assistance.

It has been shown that an athlete with high trait anxiety and experiencing the same state anxiety will find this to be debilitating to athletic performance.

How is anxiety measured in athletes?

Sports psychology has embraced the scientific method of creating a questionnaires, describing the results, then ultimately concluding that the athlete is, or isn't, anxious. The Competitive State Anxiety Inventory—2 (CSAI—2) is probably the most widely used. It can measure cognitive anxiety (the runner's fear of anxiety and negative expectations), somatic anxiety (perceptions of physiological arousal) and self-confidence. Many athletes scorn the use of such instrumentation, they don't need a pen and paper to tell them that their anxiety is holding them back.

Some researchers have attempted to explain the differences in the performances of individuals (such as the two runners in our introduction) by using the concept of "individualized zones of optimal functioning" or IZOFs. Each runner has an optimal level of pre-performance anxiety that can help produce good athletic performances. However, if the anxiety is too high or, suprisingly, too low, the performance will not be as good.

The effects of anxiety in running

A great deal of research has been devoted to the effect of anxiety on sports performance. Here are some of the findings:

- Competitive state anxiety is higher for athletes in individual sports compared with athletes in team sports.

- The more experience an athlete has, the lower the level of cognitive anxiety.

- Perceived competence and self-confidence play critical roles in the extent of anxiety experienced by the athlete. A runner who is full of self-belief is likely to be protected from the debilitating effects of anxiety. If they do experience anxiety, it is likely to have a facilitative influence.

- A cohesive sense of self esteem which is developed in childhood is thought to enable adults to cope with pressures inherent in sports. Conversely, a disordered self will fragment under extreme pressure.

- Athletes with low self-image are likely to fall into anger or despair at the first sign of difficulty.

How do you treat anxiety?

Traditional means of reducing anxiety have focused on cognitive behavioural interventions; this is a fancy way of saying: control your thoughts and change your behaviours. First, I would suggest you look for patterns; what triggers your anxiety? Does it start a few hours before the competition or is this something that can build over weeks? Clearly, the type of intervention will be moulded by your response to that question.

Next, what techniques have worked for you in the past? If the answer is none, then you might like to re-read the following articles contained in this book:
- Goal setting—read "*An action packed running career*"
- Thought control strategies such as positive thinking—read "*Tune in and tune out for a better running performance*," and "*Talking your way to success*."
- Cognitive restructuring; relaxation techniques such as diaphragmatic breathing—read "*A breath of fresh air*"
- Exercise imagery—read "*Success: it's all in your imagination*."

For most runners a defeat is nothing more than a temporary disappointment. It can either be a sobering reminder of the limits of our potential, or a jolt to make us practise that much harder. The likelihood is that most runners will be focusing on their next race or training run within a few days, with any sadness put solidly behind them. But when you are a multiple world record holder, and the hopes of the nation are resting on your shoulders, defeat carries a sharper, if not condemnatory definition. It takes a special person, indeed, a special athlete to absorb (or deflect) these pressures. This is the story of two athletes, arguably two of the greatest runners, ever. It is a story of pressure and expectation, of failure, success, and ultimately, redemption.

Redemption in Moscow

In 1980 Sebastian Coe and Steve Ovett approached the Moscow Olympic Games with reputations and honours that made them favourites for an Olympic title. The only problem was that each had the other to contend with. While history has already recorded the finishing places and times, the statistics often fail to convey the emotions, the uncertainties, and ultimately the joys of two of the greatest races in running history. What follows is a fictional account of what might have happened in the minds of these great runners as they approached two of the most eagerly anticipated running races of all time…

Gliding effortlessly over the rolling Sussex Downs (a range of hills to the south of London), Steve Ovett briefly stopped to inhale the salty breeze blowing off the South Coast. He could see and hear the sonorous waves crashing onto the beaches and it reminded him of the famous story of King Canute. Believing that he was all powerful, Canute sat on a throne and ordered the tide to stop advancing. Of course he failed and it was a jarring reminder that nobody, no matter how powerful or successful, can stop the forces of nature. Ovett reflected for a moment. He had become famous, immensely successful, and yet he understood that these moments would eventually seem like a fleeting moment in life. Time to grasp that ultimate prize: an Olympic Games title, was now. It might not ever come again. His mind closed on the idea. Many had failed where he dared to tread but he quickly dispelled any notion of failure. It had never been part of his make-up in the past. He bounced along the trail with an imperious quality in his stride, it had served him well but in the next few months would it prove to be good enough?

Ovett ran towards his coach Harry Wilson, a quiet, reflective man who had guided his talented charge with restraint. He knew only too well that Ovett's talents need but be pointed in the right direction. The effort and hard work needed to reach a supreme level of fitness came naturally to this young man. There was currently only one other runner whose talent matched Ovett's—and he too was running across hills but a few hundred miles to the north of Brighton. *"How was your run, Steve?"* *"Great, full of running, Harry."* Ovett pulled on his sweat clothes and walked off with Harry toward the car park.

Walking past a thicket, a fox suddenly darted onto Ovett's path. The fox froze; its nose twitched as if assessing opportunities or danger. Ovett looked into the creature's eyes. The fox took off at a brisk trot. *"It's a crafty animal, the fox,"* said Ovett out loud. Harry nodded. The words guile and mischief now resonated through his mind. He reflected on this chance encounter and slowly started to draw up his race plans.

The wind sweeping off the Yorkshire Moors could not stop the slim fluid form of the runner finishing off a punishing hill workout. The hills of Graves Park, Sheffield are a tough forbidding challenge for most runners but Sebastian Coe was in tremendous shape. With his coach and father, Peter Coe, holding the stopwatch, Seb moved gracefully up the incline looking as if he had just started. He finished the workout and looked down the valley. The steel mills hard at work churning out some of the toughest industrial metals in the world were an apt reminder to Coe that he would need that quality in his running.

The weeks rolled by and both runners were rounding into incredible form, however political events were unraveling that threatened to prevent this match-up from even taking place. In 1979 the Soviet Union army invaded Afghanistan and this prompted calls for a boycott of the Moscow Olympic Games. The Americans withdrew and much pressure was put on their European allies to join them. The British Prime Minister Margaret Thatcher wanted the British athletes out but recognised that the decision should rest with the British Olympic Committee. After intense lobbying on either side of the debate, it was decided to send a British team to the games; Coe and Ovett had their date with destiny confirmed!

Before they had even landed at Moscow airport, the world's press had already written the script, decided the tactics and the conclusion of each race. Coe—the invincible 800m runner—would win the Olympic 800m title. Steve Ovett, undefeated for several years would clearly win the 1500m. The bookmaker's odds were lock in step with this thinking. The British press basically expected a coronation, all that remained was the ceremony.

A place in the Olympic final seems almost guaranteed when you are the best runner in the world, but of course, there are dozens of other runners who would like to prevent that from happening. In the early rounds of the 800m, both Coe and Ovett were made to work hard for their place in the final. Two East Germans, Andreas Busse and Detlef Wagenecht, both 6 foot 6 inches tall and capable of exerting a muscular presence on the race looked particularly threatening. They made Seb Coe at 5 foot 8 inches seem almost diminutive.

This was one of the most eagerly anticipated races in Olympic history and it got off to a rather strange start. The pace for the first lap was surprisingly slow and Ovett found himself trapped in a box with the two Germans ensuring that that was where he was going to stay. Coe trailed dead last and had a distant, almost vacant look on his face. Was this part of his master plan? Moving into the 2nd lap, Coe remained last, Ovett still stuck on the inside with the Germans almost squeezing him, how could he get out of this position?

There are times when a small window of opportunity opens in a tight race. Unsettling questions scorch the brain of runners caught in a bad position: Will I make my move too soon? If I don't take this chance now will it be too late? The "what- if's" can make a confident runner indecisive. But it is at such moments that legends are born, championships won, records broken. With 250m left in this race the leader, Dave Warren from England, was starting to struggle, Kirov, the Russian sitting on his shoulder seemed poised to take the lead with the two Germans getting ready to pounce. Ovett still hugged the inside but was desparetely looking for a chance to break-out and charge for home. In a split-second that precious moment presented itself. Perhaps there was a scent of fox in the air for Ovett used all his craft and guile to seize his chance. A small gap opened between the two Germans and Ovett charged through like someone wildly swinging open a saloon bar door. He was free! Ovett poured on the speed and raced into the lead.

One can only imagine what was going through Seb Coe's mind when he saw his rival hit the front. Coe accelerated hard around the final bend but you cannot give a runner—especially one whose talent matches your own—10–15m head start and expect to catch them up the final straight. Ovett clinched victory in a decisive manner with Coe just catching the Russian Kirov on the line to claim the silver.

A silver medal at the Olympic Games would normally be the highlight of many athlete's career. It is a stunning achievement yet the despair on Sebastian Coe's face as he stepped onto the podium to receive his medal was painful to watch. In less than 2 minutes, he had gone from Coe the invincible world record holder to Coe the defeated. He had run a full 3 seconds slower than his world record time. The press—many with a hint of smug satisfaction—dipped their quills into a poisonous ink and effectively dismissed Coe's chances in the 1500m. There was no way back for this fine athlete, he had crumbled, under-performed, choked.

The poet Henry Wadsworth Longfellow once suggested that a man should aim his arrow high, for gravity will always pull it down and sometimes you will miss the mark. Coe returned several days later to contest the 1500m. He had always aimed high; it was the gold that he wanted, but now he would have to hit the target and there was no margin for error.

The early rounds of the 1500m unfolded as expected with Coe, Ovett, and a young Steve Cram (later to become world champion and mile record holder) easing through to the final. On a brilliant sunny day, they held the start line and waited. Gone was the vacant look on Coe's face, he was definitely a more determined man. Here was an athlete in search of release from his inner turmoil; here was a man in need of redemption.

The first lap saw Coe sit on the shoulders of the East German, Jurgen Straub, who ran at a controlled but steady pace. Ovett stalked his British rival looking like a fox amongst the hens. 800m passed and the pace had barely changed. It looked very much as if everyone was waiting for a last-lap burn-up, but who had the best sprint? The strength runners must have been getting nervous for suddenly, like a startled rabbit, Straub dramatically accelerated. It was a long run for home and it caught everyone off guard…everyone except for Coe and Ovett. The pace had dropped from a 63 second lap to a 54 second lap and it was exacting its toll on the rest of the field. 300m to go and Straub kicked again. Could he drop Coe? Ovett remained a stride behind Coe's shoulder. When would he strike?

Around the final bend Coe changed gears, delivered a devastating sprint and moved past Straub. He gained a 2m advantage but Ovett followed. Straub battled hard to stay with them. Coe kicked again, and again. With 50m to go he had a 3m, then 4m lead. Ovett tried to close the gap but this was not to be his day. In the last few strides, Straub inched ahead of Ovett. Coe strained for the line and the look of shock and release as he breasted the tape is one of the great sports photos in history. He had done it! He had searched his sporting soul and found himself not to be wanting.

The coronation, promised by the sporting press had occurred, but the crowns had been switched!

Sebastian Coe wins the Moscow Olympic Games 1500m

The resilient runner and a path to success

In this book you have met runners who have faced great challenges in their quest for high levels of sporting and personal success. I hope to have shown you that their paths to this success were not necessarily paved with Olympic Gold from the moment that they started to run. Certainly all of these athletes had incredible talent, but self-doubt, setback, illness or injury, or just plain misfortune have punctuated their careers...

We have seen how Roger Bannister repeatedly tried to break the four minute mile and failed. Indeed, there was the distinct possibility that John Landy would beat him to the record. Absorbing the pressures to be the first runner in history to achieve that landmark, Bannister was spurred to success by self-belief and pragmatism.

How about the tale of Steve Prefontaine seriously cutting his foot (on a broken bottle) just hours before the American University Championships (NCAA). Despite suffering incredible pain, Prefontaine destroyed the field with some aggressive front-running.

Then there is the story of Sebastian Coe, a runner who found his personal redemption in Moscow Olympic Games 1500m. Coe was then discounted as he suffered from a debilitating illness for several years. He returned, however, at the Los Angeles Olympics four years later and claimed the Olympic 1500m title—the only person in history to repeat as the 1500m champion.

Many great athletes have faded from memory when faced with a complex challenge while others have refused to yield and ended their careers on terms that they choose. Is success the quality that reinforces the will-power of these great athletes, i.e. success breeds success? Or, is there some other force that propels them to overcome obstacles and reach their goals? I would suggest that resilience is that mysterious ingredient.

The Webster's Dictionary defines resilience as *"an ability to recover from or adjust easily to misfortune or change."* How can you develop this quality?

Re-write negative beliefs

Runners who have faced repeated disappointment may start to believe that this path is one that cannot be changed. Indeed, sometimes it is easier to accept outcomes, even the setbacks, if they are somewhat predictable. A resilient runner does not accept this line of thought. Buddha once said: "Everything changes." That is one of the few constants in this complex world of ours. Making changes that will bring a different outcome starts with the thought that something new must be attempted. Psychological resilience can be developed by breaking the limiting patterns of thought that inhibit your performance. Start by writing down the erroneous belief systems that hold you back "I'm not good enough." "I'll never run that fast." "Nobody likes me," etc. Reward yourself, either through thought or something more tangible, for starting to make these changes. Let go of the doubt and vigorously pursue your new set of beliefs. Support these beliefs with committed actions: train harder or smarter, refuse to allow the comments of other people get to you. Remember that phrase "nobody can make you feel inferior without your permission!"

Learn to effectively deal with mistakes

All athletes make mistakes, either in training or racing. A resilient athlete adapts quickly, learns from their error and moves forward. This runner focuses on the effort and accentuates any positive themes that can be found in their work. An athlete that lacks this quality is likely to become depressed, frustrated, even angry. They may vent these feelings and blame others for this setback. Counselling—by either the coach or wise teammate can persuade or guide this runner towards a healthier view of their progress.

Develop self-discipline and self-control

Throughout my research for this book, it became apparent that self-discipline and self-control were key components of the champion athletes make-up. While for some people this comes naturally, I believe that these qualities can be learned and highly developed with a psychological training programme that incorporates themes discussed in this book.

I do wish you well with your training and racing. This is a fantastic sport, a healthy lifestyle choice, and I hope that this book helps to bring you all the success that you deserve.

Gary Barber

Acknowledgements

This project would not have been possible without the financial support of St. Michaels University School, Victoria, British Columbia, Canada. My sincere thanks for making this dream come true!

This book is dedicated to my family—Michelle, Michael and Colin.

The author cannot take any responsibility for any injury or illness caused as a result of the advice given within this book.

The author wishes to thank Associated Sports Photography, UK, for the right to use the photos included in this book.

Author Biography

Gary Barber is a runner with international experience on the track (1500m, sub four minute mile) and in distances up to 20 miles. He has a Masters degree in Sports Psychology and is the author of the book "Getting Started in Track and Field Athletics." His articles on sport have been published in 15 different running and triathlon magazines and numerous newspapers.

ISBN 141206556-9